PARABLES
&Parallels

Modern Day Insights into Many Ancient Words

DAVID LITWIN

PURE FUSION MEDIA
FRANKLIN, TENNESSEE

This book is dedicated to my wife and children, who supported Daddy's vision long before they understood it.

CONTENTS

The struggles here we can find across the atlas
and it all started when Adam gave up his own palace
now the earth waits for its rightful owner
2,000 years ago the second Adam told us
the kingdom is at hand,
died for the sins of man
just so He could bring us back to His original plan...
(Group 1 Crew, "Keys to the Kingdom")

I wanna take the preconceived
out from underneath your feet
dust it off and instead we'll plant some seeds
(Jack Johnson, "All at Once")

At a certain point, I just felt, you know,
God is not looking for alms,
God is looking for action.
(Bono)

SECTION 1: FOUNDATIONS

Chapter 1

WHAT ARE YOU "LEANING" ON?

Ponder:
Trust in the Lord with all your heart
And do not <u>lean</u> on your own understanding.
In all your ways acknowledge Him,
And He will make your paths straight.
(Prov. 3:5-6, NASB, emphasis mine)

The verse above is one of the most well-known and inspirational passages in the biblical text. It just may be your favorite verse, as it is with many. We love it because it tells us to trust in God with everything, and in so doing, He will make our paths, or our lives, straight or (perhaps) smooth. Like a poem, it also is very easy to memorize. It seems to flow seamlessly. If we trust and rely solely on Him, He will straighten our paths.

But we have to be aware that these words are being retranslated from their original Hebrew (Old Testament) or Greek (New Testament) texts. In the translation process, many words are replaced or their definitions are condensed.

Take, for example, the word in the second line: "lean." If I were to ask you what "leaning on your own understanding" meant, what would you say? I'll give you the most common answers I have received: "To support, to trust, to rely upon, to put faith in... your own understanding." These are very natural and logical synonyms to the word "lean." So much so that the line above even *uses* the term, "trust." So it seems like a natural progression, right? But what if I were to tell you that none of those words might describe what the author is attempting to convey with this passage? Going back to the Hebrew, here is what we find:

Lean: *Sha'an*: To lean upon one's spear in order to commit suicide.

Wow. That changes things, doesn't it? So, apart from the shock, what does that mean for us today? I hope that none of us plan to commit suicide; few of us have even seen a spear, except in museums or in the movies. So what is the modern-day relevance? The answer is an understanding of *worldviews*.

Each one of us subscribes to a set of beliefs that influences our lives and dictates our actions. Those beliefs comprise our answers to life's big questions:

How were we created?

Why are we here?

What is our purpose?

What happens to us after we die?

Our answers to these questions shape the life that we have, comprise the people that we are and determine the way we interact with others. That is called our worldview. Whether or not we are aware of it, our worldview defines us. It is that worldview, that understanding, Solomon is speaking of in the passage at the beginning of this chapter. He clearly is stating: "Do not lean on your own worldview." Why? Because of the first line: "You are resting your heart on it." Your heart, according to scripture, is the central core of your being. It is the place from which all life flows; it also is synonymous in scripture with the brain. Your heart makes up every fiber of your being.

Solomon is saying that you are resting your very being, your core essence, on your worldview, or your answers to those four questions. And those answers that you trust on or, better yet, act upon, make up a spear that is designed to run you through. It may be that you suffer physical or emotional damage because of your worldview. Perhaps, it causes you future relational pain, or generational trauma. It could be spiritual damage. Regardless, every worldview on the planet has been crafted, at some point and on some level, to run you through... except one. Reread the passage, this time with this new understanding.

> *Trust in the Lord* (the One with the true worldview) *with all of your heart* (your core essence)
> *And do not lean on the spear of your own understanding* (your worldview) (for it will surely run you through).

Just like any other worldview, the Biblical Worldview requires you to lay your heart, your very being, upon it. But in the passage above, the scripture not only acknowledges that – it encourages it! Solomon is saying, "Lean all of your core essence against the One with the true worldview, for it will PROTECT your heart, it will not destroy it." This is incredibly liberating! As a Christian, your worldview is secure from harm, and you can support every fiber of your being on its validity and protection.

But it also comes with a new sense of empathy, compassion and responsibility.

For all of those around us, those trusting in other worldviews, are not to be seen through the lens of their "immoral" actions, but through how their worldviews are harming their hearts: their bodies, minds, relationships, families and yes, their souls. Instead of attacking others for their beliefs, which really are a set of personal decisions influenced by a myriad of internal and external circumstances, we must recognize that those beliefs are producing outcomes that are in big and small ways affecting their hearts. We must speak from compassion for the essence of their being, and not merely from self-righteousness.

You are about to learn, in the coming pages, more about the power and potency of that true worldview. Let the new revelations begin.

Chapter 2

THE FORENSIC WORLDVIEW
Six Tenets That Change Everything

Ponder:
It is the glory of God to conceal a matter, but to search out a matter is the glory of kings.
(Prov. 25:2, NIV)

One of the most popular genres on network television is the forensic drama or criminal procedural. From *CSI: Crime Scene Investigation* and *NCIS* to *Cold Case* and *Criminal Minds*, Americans sit down nearly every night of the week to watch savvy criminals get bested by even savvier forensic experts, profilers and crime lab technicians. Outside the sets of Hollywood, the latest advancements in forensic tools and technologies allow police and federal agencies to study and investigate the slightest bit of trace evidence in hopes of ascertaining the nature and method of a crime and incarcerating the party responsible. Forensic technology has a purpose: to unlock the clues to a crime so that the instigating party is apprehended, often before another crime is committed.

The popularity of the forensic drama has produced a phenomenon known as the "CSI effect," a new level of savvy in the American populous that may be wreaking havoc on the criminal justice system. Jurors now expect counselors to present stronger cases of forensic evidence during court cases. Americans are looking for better evidence.

Scripture asserts that the world humanity finds itself in is a crime scene. The Bible claims that a killer runs loose in our midst, hell-bent on the destruction of mankind. But the worldview that claims this enemy is losing its popularity. Perhaps the reason is that Christians have used the Biblical Worldview theologically, apologetically and morally. But Christians have failed to use their worldview *forensically*. For like CSI, the Biblical Worldview is the only ideological system through which forensic discovery is possible.

15

All worldviews are, in the logical sense, subjective. They cannot be validated strictly within themselves, or heralded simply by their lack of theological contradiction. Despite claims to the contrary, Christians cannot prove their worldview.

But they have always been able to use it.

So how does one go about *using* a worldview? A worldview is something to "believe in," right? For most worldviews that is the case.

But not ours.

To "use" our worldview we must understand what it offers humanity. Naturally, the answer might be salvation unto heaven and a personal relationship with our Savior and Creator through the death of God's son, Jesus Christ. But as wondrous and life-altering as those realities are, the Biblical Worldview is even more expansive than that. For the Biblical Worldview differs from all other ideological systems. And because of those differences, Christianity becomes a beacon of light to the world... now. But not just in the way you might think. Below is a list of six tenets extracted from the Biblical Worldview:

1. God is the creator of all existence and humanity.
2. God made man in His image, bearing His likeness.
3. Man rejected God's plan for His creation, and, in doing so, invited evil into the world.
4. The principal head of this evil is a fallen angel named Satan, who, since his fall, seeks to "kill, steal, and destroy" those bearing God's image.
5. Satan and his forces can work through the "sons of disobedience," or prideful, fallen members of mankind, whispering inspirations and controlling systems and realms from behind the scenes, schemes most often oblivious to mankind.
6. God sent his Son into the world, to abolish the works of Satan and his evil forces, and to liberate all who believe in him from the power of sin and death, offering them eternal life after this one passes.

On the surface, these six tenets appear to have the makings of a good fantasy novel. They are neither provable nor verifiable. On their own, they must be taken on faith. But to "use" these six statements, we must extract them from scripture, or the supposedly subjective, and apply them to "reality." So how do we go about proving these supposed fantasy tenets in the real world? We begin by understanding what these six tenets offer to humanity. Let's start with the first two.

The first two tenets show that humanity was created to flourish in prosperity and benefit.

We were not simply created by an outside Force. We were created in that outside Force's image. With something we create or purchase and then possess or own, our attachment to that object is tied to our perceived value of its usefulness and its degree of expense. Therefore we can do with that object as we see fit, and we handle it according to the criteria above. We treat and operate a Ferrari very differently than we would an old clunker. That's important enough, and while many religions claim that humans also were created by an outside force, these two tenets assert we were created *in the image* of our Creator.

"God created man in His own image, in the image of God He created him; male and female He created them." (Gen. 1:27, NIV)

So our value and worth is not determined solely by the whims of our Creator; it is tied directly back to the value and worth that Creator places on Himself. Allow me to explain.

Your children are, in the most general sense, *your creation.* You do not simply possess your children, but created them directly out of your own being or essence. Children are made in the image and likeness of their biological parents. They carry their parent's learned and genetic attributes, evidenced in a mother's frustrated (or enthralled) declaration: "You are *just like* your father." Because the child is the creation of the parent, the child is, in essence, an extension of the one who created them. The term "sperm" is taken from the Greek term "sperma" or seed. Children are formed from the "seed" of their parents. The child's perceived value is therefore directly tied to the value its parent places on his or her *own* personal worth. To devalue one's children, is logically to devalue one's own existence. With ownership, value becomes tied to the individual's perception of the item owned. But with creation, value is directly correlated back to the original creator. And the more one value's oneself, the more one wishes for that which he creates in his own image to flourish and prosper. Which brings us to tenets three and four.

Man is not only made in the image of his Creator, but he bears the likeness of that Creator's enemy...

When you were in your teen years, you might have dated a person who you believed – at least at the time – was "perfect." If yours was a case similar to most teenage romances, eventually that person's perfection became greatly tarnished, usually at your expense, and customarily because another person replaced you. Inevitably, the person you were head-over-heels for became an object of scorn and anger. Obviously (at least I hope) you could not get at them physically, so you did the next best thing: *you destroyed their image.* Photos of the offending individual would be serrated, if not burned, in a violent ritualistic ceremony. This "picture demolition" attempted to fulfill the destructive tendencies brought on by revenge-oriented anger. The pictures represented the individual, so the destruction of those pictures became your best attempt at getting at him or her.

Our Creator, who has made us in His image, desires to see us prosper and flourish as His "image bearing" creation. But Satan, His enemy, wishes to see us destroyed and decimated, for the very same reason: we bear that Creator's (his enemy's) image...

For a moment I'd like you to mentally picture the one person on this planet who, like nails on a chalkboard, irritates, aggravates or frightens you like no other person can. The individual who, at the very mention of his or her name causes your fists to ball up, your muscles to tighten, your skin to crawl and sadly, maybe even your eyes to tear. Perhaps it's the greasy-haired office predator with the wandering eyes; the smelly, over-the-top relative you pray skips the family reunion; the brazen, foul-mouthed shock jock that repulses you after seeing his smug face plastered on billboards; the ex-friend that turned your afternoon chats into neighborhood gossip. Perhaps it's worse – much worse. Think about how utterly repellent this person is, how much avoiding them for the rest of your life is one of your greatest aspirations. Ponder his or her annoying traits, the strange mannerisms, those vile facial expressions or that arrogant and condescending smile. If you can, reflect on what he or she may have done to you to deserve this foul title. I'm sure by now you're utterly sick of having to relive this torturous mental picture so I'll get to the point.

Now imagine that *everyone on the planet* looked just like that person.

What if there was no place to flee from that foul, anger-producing image you so wanted to erase from your memory bank? Imagine you had to endure that image, minute by minute, day by day. It's a rather horrific thought, isn't it? This is how the enemy spoken of in tenet four sees all of mankind. For <u>everyone</u> on the planet is made in that God image. Everywhere he turns, he is faced with the image of his arch nemesis – the One whom he despises. The One he wishes to see destroyed. He can't get at his enemy, but, like the burned photograph, he can get at that enemy's image.

Therefore, <u>everyone</u> is target.

Like the claim of a global crime scene, we are ALL in the crosshairs, whether or not we acknowledge – or even believe – it. How can I be certain? After all, I claimed that it appears that these tenets must be taken on faith, correct? That's true, and I might have to leave it all at faith (or what some might simply say would be a futile hope) if that was where the tenets ended. But then we come to tenet five. So what is so critical about this fifth, supposedly fantasy tenet? This tenet shifts from the faith-laced assertions of scripture, into the tangible light of the real world. For...

Tenet five allows humanity the ability to gauge every technological, ideological, religious or philosophical offering <u>strategically.</u>

Everything created by man, from ideology to technology, starts first in the mind. Invention begins with an idea before it is ever put to paper or implemented into society. So if there exists an enemy capable of whispering into the mind of the human Creator, as these tenets assert, then everything created can be studied to determine whether it has been designed, in some big or small way, for prosperity and flourishing (the desire of our Creator) or for destruction (the despotic intent of Creator God's enemy). Not through its human inventor's claims of purpose or use. And not just through its moral or spiritual implications.

But *through its outcomes.*

So far this has ALL been highly esoteric. So below is a small list of creations that are considered both for intended purpose <u>and</u> objective outcome:

Crystal meth was created for the intended purpose of euphoria, *but its objective outcome includes serious brain defects and the loss of crucial brain chemicals, the deterioration of the body, the loss of sleep and food intake. Not to mention near-instantaneous biological addiction.*

The intended purpose of promiscuous sex is physical and psychological elation, *but the objective outcome can be venereal disease, cervical cancer, AIDS, depression and infertility.*

The intended purpose of alcohol is physiologic stimulation, *but its objective outcome can include depression, addiction, internal organ damage and, if driving is added, incarceration for DUI or worse: manslaughter.*

The (somewhat) intended purpose of gambling is having a good time and potentially winning big, *but the objective outcome is bankruptcy, poverty, the loss of job or family, depression and anxiety.*

The intended purpose of pornography is sexual stimulation, *but the objective outcome can be erectile dysfunction, divorce, depression and possibly even incarceration if children are involved.*

The world is confounded by the debilitating outcomes of its actions, many of which are seen as humanity's greatest "freedoms" (such as promiscuous sexuality). But the believer, equipped with these six tenets, can begin to see the outcomes of these actions, not as frustrating byproducts, but as their strategic intent. We can proclaim from the rooftop that alarming statistics of disease, addiction, alcoholism, depression and anxiety, STDs, etc., are not just the unconnected result of certain actions; they are the *intent* of these actions. God desires prosperity for humanity, his greatest creation. The enemy seeks to destroy that creation. And we can see the interplay of both desires occur through *the outcomes* of our actions.

A brilliant doctor friend of mine has begun to look at diabetes not as a disease, but as a pathway toward its final intent. Diabetes leads to blindness, loss of limbs, heart disease and attack, stroke and other serious ailments. He now is attempting to get the medical community to associate these outcomes with the metaphor of a predator, such as a lion. Diabetes is not a disease; it's a strategy. And poor dieting (or what Dante would call the sin of gluttony) and lack of exertion (what Dante would call the sin of slothfulness) do not just lead to diabetes. They are pathways toward the purpose of consuming your body parts and ultimately taking your life. In America today, there are more than 60 million people who are highly subject to diabetes. These people might act one way if they consider diabetes a disease with some dangerous but unintended side effects. They might act entirely differently if they consider that the outcomes are the very purposed intent of the initial actions.

But for all of the transformative power of his revelation, for all the benefit it is having with his patients and those who hear his lectures, he only could have come to that revelation through the worldview of the six tenets presented above.

For no other worldview can look at the world *strategically.*

All other religions claim an enemy that exists *inside* of mankind, an enemy that is a portion of mankind (such as Israel to Islam), or is some missed attribute humanity has yet to evolve into, such as human ignorance and religious dogmatism (humanism) or un-enlightenment (many Eastern religions). Based on the foundational tenets of ALL other worldviews, there is no ultimate plan and purpose to our world, nor is there ultimate resistance. Therefore to all other worldviews, what happens in the world is simply happenstance. It is tragic, confounding and even caustic, but it is happenstance nonetheless. But claiming an enemy OUTSIDE of mankind, with the capacity to INFLUENCE mankind, humanity was given the authority to "question" society's alarming statistics. Only the Biblical Worldview allows us to hold everything up to the spotlight and see what also might be hidden in the shadows, to look at anything mankind has created, and state, "Maybe something bigger is at play" than just man's inventiveness. Armed with these six tenets, we have an answer for the world's puzzling tragedies, for we deliberately can equate initial actions with future consequences. It is as if God Himself is sitting like Morpheus in the high-backed chair and inviting us to see how deep the rabbit hole goes.

Let me give you a more detailed example. I have a friend who was involved in local government while living in Florida. Florida is known for its "gentlemen's clubs;" they are a big business in that state. But she knew that this was not only wrong in God's eyes; it also was harming her community. So instead of picketing the local establishments or holding church rallies or prayer meetings to combat the "evil" in her community, she did research... lots and lots of research. She found out that around a fixed circumference of gentlemen clubs, on a national level, there was more crime per capita than areas without these clubs. She discovered that alcoholism in families increased around these clubs. Education, also, suffered in areas surrounding these clubs. And family issues and divorce were more frequent when these clubs moved into the area. Instead of focusing on actions, *she researched outcomes.*

She then created an aggressive campaign, targeting these key issues to the local constituents in her district. Bottom line, they removed the gentlemen's clubs in the district. What a victory for God, right? Sin removed, purity restored? That's one way to look at it. But what also about the victory for the safety of the people in the area; the loss of addiction; the increase in educative potential; and the strengthening of the family, because she used the lens of the Biblical Worldview to help her community, helping it prosper and thrive as God intended?

Are church rallies and prayer events critical? Of course. But they often fail to translate to effective action in the eyes of the general populous.

THE FAILURE OF THE FAITHFUL

As the church, we often think far too myopically. Instead of *using* our worldview, we have attempted to prove it and lord it over others. Rather than exposing and healing humanity from its *outcomes*, we have attacked humanity for its *actions*. The world continues to suffer, and the only worldview capable of exposing strategies against mankind is pushed further and further to the fringes. Christianity, at least in the eyes of the culture, often fails humanity for the sake of proving itself.

But the purpose is not just the validation of the worldview; it is for the concern, protection and guardianship of mankind. If the world is a crime scene as scripture claims, then humanity is the target. The end result is legion, but to trace the pathway of these strategies requires more than scripture. It requires real and tangible action and education in the real world. We as believers, equipped with this understanding that the world's troubling statistics aren't merely happenstance, need to understand how to use science, education, media, government and the family to provide the healing ointment (which you will soon discover how to apply), where the world can only offer weak substitutes (which you also soon will discover).

Rescue those being led away to death.... (Prov. 24:11, NIV)

It is God's image (mankind) that must be the central focus of the need for forensic investigation. And every human being, from the ardent atheist, to the pornographer, to the drug dealer to the radical Islam militant, still bears that image. Scripture makes it clear and I will soon further clarify: our battle is not with flesh and blood. Man, whether he instigates the actions or suffers the effects, is thrust under the consequence of systems, technologies and ideologies unintentionally developed for the sake of his destruction and stagnation. And you will soon discover that the initial benefit of many of these offerings is merely the catalyst toward their intended destructive application.

While salvation is the ultimate solution for humanity, and Jesus is the final physician (the glorious reality of tenet six), that isn't always the first step to a hurting culture. Our worldview is so expansive that it encapsulates ALL of existence. For we, as believers equipped with these six tenets, have the lens by which to discover the strategies against humanity, but the world has many of the tools to rectify the aftermath. We must learn how to look at scientific, sociological, psychological and medicinal findings objectively. And, as you will discover in future chapters, we must use these findings in wisdom-infused ways to come up with real solutions to our world's problems. Our goal must be the bodies and minds of those around us, not simply their souls.

Before we tell them our worldview is better, let's <u>show</u> them something better first. What did Jesus say?

"Taste and see." Not, "hear and learn."

The world can, at best, see its biggest issues "through a glass darkly," but it can not directly connect action to consequence. We can. And we must. If we are going to transform our western world, we must recognize that we have been given even more than a pathway into heaven. We have been given the "keys to the Kingdom." We just need to recognize exactly what they open.

Chapter 3

DEBUGGING A FALLEN WORLD

Ponder:
The Lord God commanded the man, saying... from the tree of the knowledge of good and evil you shall not eat....
(Gen. 2:16-17, NASB)

And you shall again obey the Lord, and observe all His commandments which I command you today.
(Deut. 30:8, NASB)

Have you ever stopped to ponder why a God who asserted He was the same "yesterday, today and forever," would give mankind a single commandment in the garden and then 613 commandments in the desert? One of the main arguments against the Christian faith is that its supreme Deity is controlling, subjugating and restrictive. Instead of liberating humanity to explore its full potential, the deity Jehovah (JHVH) stifles man, forcing him to perform inside a narrow pathway of moral confinement. Many claim that we serve a God who cordons mankind into a pleasure-squelched life of do's and don'ts. Consider the following quote by ardent atheist Richard Dawkins:

> *The God of the Old Testament is arguably the most unpleasant character in all fiction: jealous and proud of it; a petty, unjust, unforgiving control-freak... megalomaniacal, sadomasochistic, capriciously malevolent bully.* (*The God Delusion*, p51, condensed for emphasis)[1]

But if Jehovah's (JHVH) intent was man's restriction and deprivation, at the onset of humanity He certainly wasn't a very demagogic taskmaster. The single restriction for mankind (found in the verse in Genesis above) probably had a radius of somewhere around 60 feet. Other than an action originating on an infinitesimal point on the

25

globe (inside the reach of the limbs and branches of the tree of knowledge of good and evil) man was given no other boundaries. If God were the same, yesterday, today and forever as He claims, then his first intent would always be His ultimate intent. Simple logic dictates that if you are an unchanging being, then your first action is always your *intended* action.

So if God doesn't change, then... why the change?

Why go from man's nearly limitless freedom to His supposedly constricting confinement. Why outstretch and then snatch back? Why go from one simple law, to more than 600 painfully exacting mandates?

Answering that question does not require us to step back in time. Nor does it necessitate some theoretical exercise or deep theological treatise. It requires only a journey into the objective present. Using a present-day phenomenon, propagated through approximately the last 50 years – and more specifically the last 10 – we can unlock the reason for the introduction of the new mandates. It was not God who had changed. Nor was it ultimately man that was altered. Instead, the surrounding physical environment had been changed. And that change both determined – and caused – every decision to follow.

COMPUTER PROGRAMMING 101

When a computer programmer or programming team develops a new coding language (PHP, DOS, XML, etc.), the created coding system becomes a new world through which its participants must now operate. If its creators are brilliant enough, inside the boundary of a new programming language there is immense freedom and opportunity for growth. Depending on the competency and diligence of the future users of a new coding system, great and mighty feats can be accomplished, feats so extraordinary they often cause the original authors to marvel at the distances these new users can take their systems.

Today, many of our coding systems allow general users, those without detailed knowledge of the programming language, to make changes, improvements and additions to its applications and programs. It is known as *open source programming*. Riding the Internet wave of autonomy and accessibility, open source programming languages nearly have become industry standard. Wikipedia describes open source as that which "allows concurrent input of different agendas, approaches and priorities." It creates a highly favorable and usable architecture for individuals who have little desire or time to learn the programming language. But for those who dedicate themselves to learning these open source languages, a greater and richer experience occurs. These dedicated users are able to develop far more spectacular creations than the average user. This minimal-maximal methodology makes open source a highly desirous and profitable platform. As Linus Torvalds, the Finnish software engineer and developer of the Linux kernel, stated: "The future is open source everything."

Ironically, it isn't the future that will usher in an open source utopia. Instead, open source originated out of the very distant past.

BACK... TO THE BEGINNING

In the biblical story of creation, we learn that everything God created worked symbiotically with everything else around it. Light was created before dirt, which was created before plants – so that the plants could flourish in the ground and photosynthesize through the light, producing oxygen for the animals soon to follow and so on and so forth. So according to the Bible, when God first placed man in the garden, (metaphorically) the "software" running the physical world was flawless. Inside this flawless system, the Creator allowed His creation to independently develop and create. He blessed them and told them to continue building upon the initial system.

> *Be fruitful and multiply, and fill the earth, and subdue it…*
> (Gen. 1:28, NASB)

When man was given authority to operate according to his own agenda, God created the first open source system. Man was encouraged to add to the created system, to craft his own path through the established software. We now can see why liberty was so liberally granted. The freedom of the flawless system granted freedom to man. There was nothing running through the perfect software system that could damage the system (and therefore man)… except one.

> *"[B]ut from the tree of the knowledge of good and evil you shall not eat, for in the day that you eat from it you will surely die."*
> (Gen. 2:17, NASB)

Taken strictly from a theological viewpoint, this appears to be the first moral commandment. But stepping back into the realm of software programming unveils why this restriction had to stand. It was not a restriction against humanity's freedom. It was the single restraint necessary _for_ humanity's freedom.

PROGRAMMING... AND ITS PROBLEMS

I stated prior that inside the boundaries of any well-developed programming language there is immense freedom. And depending on the competency and diligence of its programmers, great and mighty feats can be accomplished. But entrenched in the strata of every coding language are pitfalls. The nature of the language opens it up for failure.

When a programmer creates an application or program, the interaction between lines of code can produce serious errors and complications. These debilitating errors aren't just glaring coding mistakes. They can manifest when one section of perfectly articulated code inadvertently clashes with another.

A single error in a line of code can propagate errors in past lines of code, leading to future problems, and... well, it all becomes a huge mess really quickly. In the programming world, debilitating coding errors are known as "bugs."

Stepping back a few decades, the nerd-cult film _TRON_ featured a humorous interaction with "bugs." As a single bug populated on a minute portion of the computer landscape, a host of new bugs sprung up around it. Any computer programmer in the theater could be heard riotously laughing. They understood the connection. A single bug in a line of computer code can cause all previously written code, and even any future coding, to be rendered inoperable. Because of the nature of bugs, errors don't always manifest right away, causing the programmer countless tens – if not hundreds or thousands – of hours of additional frustration.

THE NECESSITY OF "DEBUGGING"

Naturally, a programmer starts with an intentional purpose for his or her application or program. In order to ensure that his "creation" operates according to his intentions, a computer programmer must first "debug" that code. Debugging is the slow and painstaking process of isolating areas of incorrectly programmed code and/or determining what lines of code might be conflicting with other code. Although programming languages allow for immense autonomy and future growth, they can, through the proliferation of bugs, ruin everything previously created. Only after a program has been debugged is it fully ready to accomplish its creator's intended purpose.

For whatever reason (time, selfishness, lack of creativity, etc.) a creator may allow bugs to plague his or her intended program. But in doing so, his or her creation is severely gelded of its power and potency. At its worst, the program is rendered completely inoperable. More importantly, the program's power loss and extreme difficulty does not necessarily affect the initial programmer. Instead the difficulty is thrust upon its future users and programmers. A computer program or application that still is infested with bugs at the time of its release often faces a seriously limited shelf life. Think Microsoft Vista, filled with so many bugs that most of the PC community rejected it and forced Microsoft to build Windows 7.

AFTER THE FALL

When man "sinned" in the garden, it was not merely man's first moral failure requiring some form of moral restitution. It had little to do with the act itself. It was even more severe. Humanity had been more than separated from its Creator. Instead, the open source software system running the earth and the universe was ripped open and exposed to the immense possibility and probability of bugs. The tree of the knowledge of good and evil was a portal, a door holding back millions of carnivorous cockroaches that once unleashed, would be nearly impossible to control. The new bugs in the system had been unleashed on all humanity, on nature and on the physical universe itself. They were given immense, albeit unintended, authority to shatter, decimate and annihilate all the components functioning inside the system. God hadn't changed. Instead, His whole open source system was now affected.

So what were these bugs? The common, standard theological answer would be "sin." But such an answer fails to understand the magnitude of just what happened through the fall...

Sin, on its own, is not the only tragedy of man's fall. The other tragedy, and the most immediately damaging bug in the software system, is entropy. Entropy is the principle that all physical forms are (now) in the process of breakdown. That erosion, decay and failure are the standards by which the software system is now governed. We see the effects of entropy through the line of Adam, as the life span of successive descendants grew shorter and shorter. But it is through the understanding of entropy that we discover how sin gets its power.

And through entropy we uncover a new purpose of sin.

ENTROPY, DEATH AND PLEASURE

After the fall, death, decay and decomposition were inevitable. Death had been given an unintended authority, but its timetable WAS NOT predetermined. Although death now controlled the final outcome, man isn't going to deliberately run to death. Strategically, death and entropy needed a mechanism, a conduit to mislead and entrap humanity into willingly opening the gates of destruction, decay and decomposition.

That gateway was pleasure and feeling-based living.

Pre-fall, God had given humanity the ability to experience pleasure, even crafted the human body with various erogenous zones. But after the fall, *pleasure could be used a weapon.* Pleasure was no longer free. Man's physical and emotional feelings now could betray him. What God had designed as a gift for humanity, pleasure, became a mechanism for his demise. Man had been thrust into a world of endless possibility – and endlessly uncertain outcome. Man didn't experience freedom after the fall; instead, he now was bound by the "freedom" of his actions. But pleasure itself wasn't the culprit; it was based on how and when pleasure was engaged.

THINKING DEEPER

Both the Christian cohort and the humanist camp tend to focus on the initial actions of sin, whether that sin is promiscuous sexual activity, drug usage, pornography, drunkenness or the like. The Humanist scoffs at the Christian for denying himself the pleasures that make us human, while the Christian bellows back, "God said these actions are sin and you will be judged for your unrighteousness!" Both sides have missed this strategic understanding.

Though pleasure may be man's starting and ending point for certain "sinful" actions, it is not the goal of sin. The Christian often runs from addressing the pleasurable aspects of sin. But it only is because sin is pleasurable that it can accomplish its intended goal. Sin uses pleasure (the lust of the eyes, the lust of the flesh and the pride of life) strictly as its inciting mechanism. It is the lure through which to draw in its unsuspecting quarry. Something as euphoric as physiologic pleasure must be sin's inciting mechanism...

... because sin may begin with pleasure, but its intent is to end with entropy.

Through the law of entropy women eventually grow infertile. But using the euphoric pleasure of "sinful" promiscuous sex as the mechanism, a woman that contracts a sexually transmitted disease may face the entropic effects of infertility at the age of 22, not 46. Through the law of entropy, the brain eventually will begin to atrophy as a human continues to age. But using the pleasurable effects of the "sinful" narcotic XTC as the mechanism, sin forces a 16-year-old boy to endure the entropy-originated brain chemistry of a 60-year-old man. Through the law of entropy, dimentia and dizzy spells eventually overtake the aged or sick. But using the pleasurable but "sinful" state of drunkenness as the mechanism, a 30-year-old man can get behind the wheel of a vehicle under a similar form of dementia, strike a tree, hit the windshield with his forehead, cause a brain hemorrhage and launch another facet of the law of entropy.

Through the law of entropy the heart eventually can fail. But using the pleasure of "sinful" gluttonous eating as the mechanism, sin forces the heart of an overweight overeater to endure far more pressure than it ever intended, causing it to arrest at 38 rather than 87. Through the law of entropy, on a genetic level, a baby can be born with debilitating birth defects and diseases. But using the pleasurable enticement of "sinful" alcohol or narcotics as the inciting mechanism, hundreds of thousands more babies are born with unintended birth defects. Through entropy man will eventually die. But sin, using power, greed and pride as the inciting mechanism, caused more than six million Jews – men, women and children – to face ultimate entropy well before ultimate entropy would have occurred.

We now can unveil a new portion of sin's strategic nature:

Sin, using pleasure as its inciting mechanism, forces humanity to engage the laws of entropy faster than the system naturally intended.

Forced entropy becomes the ultimate destructive bug, ransacking everything existing inside the system. Like a single line of bugged software code, one action can cause a calculated chain reaction wreaking havoc on all the components of the system. After the fall, the cataclysmic bugs of natural entropy populated the software system, capitalized on by sin to produce unnatural, expedited or forced entropy specifically to weaken and destroy the system's internal creations faster than the system intended.

NEVER CHANGING

But God is still the "same, yesterday, today and forever." He still wanted humanity to experience life as He intended – pre-fall in freedom, not post-fall in capitalized destruction. The system had not only been disrupted; it also had been turned upside down, using one of God's greatest gifts (pleasure) to cause the acceleration. The bugs that now propagated the system used mankind's nature against him, for the purpose of his own destruction. Now, if God is unchanging, then His open source system could and would continue to run as planned. But it was no longer impervious to the maliciousness of these bugs.

To circumvent entropy would require the Creator to intervene on the system itself. But in doing so, His system no longer would remain open source. In other words, God would have gone against His own predisposed nature to eliminate the bugs in the system.

But the new bugs of forced entropy were not a new standard of the system; they were a strategy. And that strategy was weakening and destroying his greatest creation. Therefore, by writing new lines of code into the open source system through His creation (mankind), forced entropy could be cordoned.

When God went from one law in the garden to 613 laws in the desert, he was not restricting humanity with new legislation. He was recoding the system to circumvent the entropic bugs that were using pleasure to produce forced entropy. What seemed like moral, dogmatic, restrictive ordinances was a loving, unchanging Creator debugging a now-flawed system for the sake of a creation (humanity) forced to operate through the system's brokenness and destructive strategies.

SIMPLIFIED...

We can break it down simply by saying that man, since the fall, has wanted freedom in his actions – but he now is bound to its outcome. And once outcome wreaks havoc on man, man is no longer free with his future actions. The outcome of sinful pleasures that incite entropy geld man's ability to participate in the fullness of life individually, societally and historically.

But God was concerned with *freedom in outcome*, because it kept man free to engage in future action and therefore prosper exponentially. God restricted humanity from actions that had *the propensity* to produce damaging outcome which in turn would create future bondage and geld man of future action and prosperity.

LIBERATION!

God wasn't restricting humanity; he once again was liberating him! Because the purpose of debugging the system was not only for the benefit of what was in the system, but also for the ultimate *potential* of what was in that system. Unfettered to outcome, man can live a life of vitality, prosperity and holistic wholeness. He can live up to his full potential. God is not restrictive or dogmatic. His "freedom for humanity" nature never changed. Instead, He was protecting humanity from all of the cataclysmic personal, social and historical outcome that followed forced entropy.

A QUICK EXAMPLE

Let's look at one of God's most seemingly dogmatic and seemingly maniacal declarations. Consider the following two commandments.

If a man commits adultery with another man's wife... both the adulterer and the adulteress are to be put to death. (Lev. 20:10, NIV)

To that we'll add the following statute:

If a man has sexual relations with an animal, he is to be put to death, and you must kill the animal. (Lev. 20:15, NIV)

Based on the first commandment, it might seem understandable how one could perceive God as dictatorial, unloving, extreme and intolerant. After all, they were told to put the person *to death* for committing adultery? Today committing adultery *isn't even a crime,* let alone an action *worthy of extermination.* On the surface these statutes appear inhumane and certainly illiberal. This supposed "intolerance" drives many people away from following the Creator of these laws.

But this is because mankind has failed to understand sin's intent of forced entropy. But God, since He *created mankind,* fully understood both the laws of entropy and the intent of sin. To see this, we simply need to play out the failure to enforce these laws from a non-moral perspective.

By allowing the Israelites to engage in extramarital activity, God would have allowed them a primary transmission point of disease. Maybe the people would only contract and transmit moderate diseases from promiscuous sexual activity. Now factor in the man who engages in sexual relations with an animal, and contracts a life-altering (not to mention life-eradicating) disease. Because promiscuous sex is allowed, the life-threatening disease he now carries passes quickly through the nation, resulting in forced entropy on a large majority of the society.

> *A city which goes forth a thousand strong Will have a hundred left...*
> (Amos 5:3, NASB)

Are these two laws *too extreme* now? Or do we need to remind ourselves of the *millions* that have died or are dying from AIDS, the *tens of millions* of orphan children (soon to be an estimated 20 million in Africa alone) around the world who have lost their parents to the disease, and the hundreds of *billions* spent on AIDS research and medicine? All to find a cure to something that never would have occurred had our "advanced" society followed the rules outlined by God's "harsh" and "inhumane" commandments? Without adherence to God's law structure, sin, using pleasure as the mechanism and entropy as the intent, has the "freedom" to run *its* course unhindered. Through an animosity toward religious hypocrisy and an embrace of humanistic secularism, we've "advanced" beyond our ability to protect ourselves.

A QUICK, BUT CRITICAL, CAVEAT

Now, do not assume that this means we are to grab the nearest stones and pummel the sexual infidels living among us or reintroduce ceremonial law into our modern culture. God gave mankind the laws, not strictly to enforce them, but through their initial enforcement to understand and then expose the strategy of sin. God was attempting to unveil to mankind the conspiracy that had gripped him from the moment Adam sinned in the garden. The protection of the law was to expose the STRATEGY of sin, not to be used to lord it over others. Consider the following scenario from Jesus' life.

HE WHO IS WITHOUT SIN....

The teachers of this law (and therefore those that should have understood these strategies) brought to Jesus a woman who was caught in the act of adultery. The law we just spoke of commanded that this woman be stoned. It was God's ordinance, part of His plan for debugging the fallen world. And yet Jesus stated, "He who is without sin, cast the first stone," and left her forgiven and free. What happened? Did God's nature change? Absolutely not. Then is Jesus a kindler, gentler version of the supposedly harsh, maniacal God of the Old Testament? To answer that question is to view Jesus' actions from an entirely new perspective.

If the goal of God's ordinances was the protection and liberation of humanity, then the system had to be followed perfectly. Entropy is not subjective; it is a very real, very dogmatic part of the fallen world. God only was dogmatic when He came up against the dogmatic and tangible outcome of sin and death.

If the teachers of the law were engaged in the same sins, and had relegated these actions to mere moral failures, then stoning the girl would have no effect on God's intended system of protection and liberation for humanity. In other words, without following the debugging system to the letter, the teachers of the law's focus was predominantly a moral code. And as a moral code it was not only gelded of its intent, but it also could no longer point back to its initial Creator. But it was never about the letter of the law; it was about unveiling the God through whom the law offered liberation and prosperity to humanity.

GOD'S INTENDED VISION

Once humanity recognized the prosperity found in the system, and that system pointed back to its original Creator, man would give up his futile and destructive quest for sinful pleasures. Not because the actions weren't pleasurable, but because man now understood the strategy against him. Pleasure isn't evil, but pleasure, engaged in outside of God's debugging system, was being weaponized. God didn't restrict man from pleasure, only pleasure acted upon at the wrong time or in the wrong fashion – so that it caused entropy and destruction. Once mankind finally made this connection between sin, pleasure and entropy, man didn't need the law to control his life. He would follow it willingly, because to not follow it not only meant his demise, but also the loss of his time, talent and treasure through dealing with the effects of entropy individually, societally and historically. And that knowledge led man to back to further intimacy with his Creator.

THE CHURCH

And yet still today, the very ones (the church) that are supposed to be the ambassadors of this debugging system often use it as little more than a moral code. It is a moral code containing little power (even over its own people), and with no semblance of its intended effect on all of humanity. This moral code not only limits the purposed intent of the law, but it also distances humanity away from its Creator. And for much of society, it appears to relegate the Old Testament God to

Dawkins' description of a *"petty, unjust, unforgiving control-freak... megalomaniacal, sadomasochistic, capriciously malevolent bully."*

But thankfully we now can uncover an even greater significance to this debugging system... *through the role of Jesus.*

JESUS – THE <u>ULTIMATE</u> NEO

After the fall, God's system was riddled with bugs. Those bugs deliberately were destroying humanity. In God's love, He offered humanity a way to debug the system, should they have chosen it. But man, still motivated by pleasure and wracked with outcome, did not adhere to God's debugging system. The software continued to remain damaged, yet God <u>still</u> "loved the world." He still wanted humanity to operate in freedom, prosperity and liberation. But if His nature never changed, He still would not affect the system from the outside. So God logically could do one other thing. He could step *into* His own coding system. Not as God from the outside, but from the inside as part of His creation. If He were to enter the system, He would adhere to both its open source makeup and His own self-imposed mandate.

God, from the inside, could enter into the system and take authority against all the bugs that were wreaking havoc on humanity.

> *[B]ecause through Christ Jesus the law of the Spirit of life who gives life has set you free from the law of sin and death.* (Rom. 8:2, NIV)

Or, we can retranslate this now to say: "Through Jesus, the new programming language of life also sets me free of the post-fall programming of sin and death." Jesus stepped into the system, to set the system back "to rights." He pulled the full power of the bugs onto himself and defeated their overarching control over the system! By entering into the bugged system for the sake of its debugging, He could express His love for humanity and its liberation without affecting His nature:

> *Do not think that I have come to abolish the Law or the Prophets; I have not come to abolish them but to fulfill them.* (Matt. 5:17, NIV)

God wasn't restricting humanity through His supposedly subjugating law. He was liberating humanity to reach its full potential. And Jesus wasn't just saving humanity from sin. He was once and for all recoding the bugged programming that had combined sin and death (or entropy) into a cataclysmic concoction of bondage-laden outcome.

In Jesus, the software creator became its most prolific programmer. Jesus also sacrificed himself so that the system could once again be set to rights, and He now calls each of us to do our part to finish what He started, to finish debugging the system. God's Son started the task; God's image is to finish it.

The church, His programming ambassadors, is not to debug by just enforcing the law, but by unveiling the strategies that the law illuminated!

... *[F]or before the law was given, sin was in the world. <u>But sin is not taken into account when there is no law.</u>* (Romans 5:13 NIV, emphasis mine)

The system still remains open source; man must make his own choice. But riddled with the deliberate consequences of sin, the church can show that his choice is either for his own prosperity, or his immediate or eventual demise.

The church's role now shifts from being (in part) God's moral police, to the purveyors of mankind's liberation and exposers of the strategies against mankind. Its goal is to love and serve humanity through its pain of entropic outcome, not to condemn it for falling prey to its own pleasure-based nature. This is part of the true nature of love. And "God so loved the WORLD..."

God has not only been a God of love, but also a God whose very desire is to see mankind reach its full potential, to operate through God's original intent. Throughout history, first through His law and then through His Son, He has sought to debug the system, to set humanity back on its intended course, free from the strategies of sin and death and able to experience man's full potential.

SO WHAT NOW?

Through this new understanding I believe the call to the church (God's primary ambassadors) is threefold:

First, it must recognize and broadcast that God's nature is to protect and prosper humanity – not just the church. God loves all made in His image and grieves when it suffers under the bugs and the strategies of this fallen world.

Second, the church must shift its focus strictly from speaking about sin to understanding and revealing the STRATEGIES of sin, uncovering how sin has used our very human nature as a weapon against us for the sake of our own destruction. The church needs to shift from promoting morality (simply THAT He said something) to understanding WHY God has said what He said and done what He has done. By focusing on outcome, it can begin to show the culture a new form of love and offer empathetic solutions to the cataclysmic effects of pleasure-distorted entropy.

Third, the church must take up its role of debugging the world, both in educating the culture to the strategies against it, and then in using everything in its power to eradicate the effects of forced entropy on humanity. As you will soon read, it needs to use its spiritual arsenal to address these issues. But also through science, medicine, psychology, government, the arts, media, humanities, etc., it must understand how to do its part to lessen entropy and sin's powerful hold on humanity. Instead of attempting to take the "Seven Mountains of Culture," it must use those mountains to broadcast these strategies to the world and unveil wisdom-infused plans to see them alleviated. Doing so will begin to create a prosperous society once again, free from the binding shackles of entropy and sin.

And finally, it must present a loving God and His glorious Christ as the liberator that He truly is, offering others the opportunity to join in the great adventure of debugging this fallen world.

... *[W]here the Spirit of the Lord is, there is freedom.* (2 Cor. 3:17, NIV)

1. Dawkins, Richard, The God Delusion, Great Britain: Bantam Press, 2006. Print.

Chapter 4

THE LAND OF BEES AND COWS

Ponder:
*He brought us to this place and gave us this land,
a land flowing with milk and honey....*
(Deut. 26:9, NIV)

One of the most critical components of a corporation's overall brand message is its marketing slogan or pitch. Hundreds, if not thousands of hours went into seemingly simplistic phrases such as: "The Best a Man Can Get," (Gillette); "I'm Loving It," (McDonalds); or "What Can Brown Do for You?" (UPS). Comprised of just a few words, these slogans are crafted and re-crafted again and again, honed to perfection with the knowledge that the final statement the company chooses will represent the broadly diverse aspects of the corporation's culture, products and services. It is not a fly-by-night exercise, but a strategic and calculated procedure with massive internal and external significance. The wrong brand slogan, the wrong corporate message, can seriously debilitate a corporation. But the right slogan can rocket a company's brand awareness and corporate sales far past its competitors.

When God marketed the Promised Land to His chosen people the Israelites, He too gave the land its own marketing slogan. He described it as a land "flowing with milk and honey." Let's stop and think for just a moment. Supposedly the God that created the entire universe, and crafted and controls all language, is giving His personal best marketing pitch for the most prime real estate on the planet. And how does He describe the location?

Taken at face value: *It was the land of bees and cows.*

Now, honey was a valuable and delectable commodity. Solomon, slated as the wisest man to ever have lived, metaphorically compared honey to wisdom, and then went on to claim that wisdom was of "more worth than gold." In some ancient civilizations, bees were revered over slaves. Honey certainly was a food of luxury, and well known for its health-imbuing qualities. In ancient Egypt, more than 500 medicinal remedies were honey-based.

Milk is also a valuable necessity. The central ingredient found in all dairy products is obviously milk. At the time, milk was probably bacterially safer than drinking water. So both descriptors hold value. But why did God specifically and repeatedly refer to their future residence as the land of bees and cows? Obviously "the land of milk and honey" sounds a bit more inviting, but it doesn't take a rocket scientist to correlate the byproduct with the product.

There certainly were other distinctive qualifiers He could have chosen. After all, the first time a small band of Israel's leaders entered the land, they brought back monstrous grapes from their 40-day survey. Why not call it the land "overflowing with wine," since that would already have resonated with the people? Or perhaps He could have called it the land of "endless salmon." If I had been in control of the marketing pitch, I might have referred to it as "the land of countless gold and precious stones." After all, that was enough of a marketing slogan for the original Spanish and French explorers to sell all their possessions, kiss family and friends farewell, and venture off past the uncharted horizon with no prior knowledge of their sail route and a miniscule chance of surviving for the return voyage. Just what was God thinking? The land of bees and cows?

It would seem that in His infinite wisdom and understanding of the craft of language (after all, He invented it) He could have used a much more powerful metaphorical descriptor. I mean, let's get real. Was the populace that inhabited the geography prior to the Israelites bragging to their nation's neighbors that their land sported ubiquitous bovines and endless bee's nests?

One might speculate that this was a common distinction to describe a good land, but no other prior geographic locale was described in such a manner. We have no other previously recorded text that has used that descriptor either. More strikingly, it was God himself who authored its first introduction into language at the burning bush, *"to bring them up from that land to a good and spacious land, to a land flowing with milk and honey."* (Ex. 3:8, NASB)

It also is highly unlikely that the Israelites themselves understood the context behind the verbal pitch. During a low point in the desert journey, two defiant brothers came against Moses and described their former slave land of Egypt as "flowing with milk and honey." Had they understood its context, they would never have used such a description. Attempting to associate their former land with God's verbal description of their "inheritance" caused the earth to open up and swallow those men and their entire clan alive. Their "inheritance" was much more than the land of bees and cows. Though the Israelites stumbled and grumbled through the desert clueless about its meaning, God was laser-accurate in His description. For the only two items on the entire planet that symbolically correlate His intended message for His people's inheritance are: "milk and honey."

Let's go back to what we learned in the last chapter for a moment. God designed the world in a perfect, pre-fall state. He designed man in that state, to live forever through eating from the tree of life. Man rejected that system, and so was thrust into a world full of sin and entropy. Man now endured life in a "post-fall" world. But what did we learn next? God, in His infinite love, wanted to redeem man back to his pre-fall state. He couldn't change the system, couldn't rewrite the code. So He gave humanity, through the Israelites, a new set of code designed to circumvent the post-fall laws of sin and death in the best pre-fall manner possible. God's intent was to create the very best pre-fall solution for humanity now living inside of a post-fall world.

God's original intent for humanity was for man to live forever, but his new opportunity for humanity was for man to live as optimally and prosperously as he could inside of this now post-fall world.

MORE THAN BEES AND COWS

The U.S Department of Agriculture every year releases its daily food group intake recommendations for Americans. It is easily compiled for mass-market adoption in the form of a food pyramid. On the bottom of the pyramid is found the bread, cereal, rice and pasta group. The department recommends between six and 11 servings of these high-carb items per day. On the second rung of the pyramid are fruits and vegetables. The recommended daily allowance (RDA) is two to four servings and three to five servings, respectively. Traveling up the pyramid, we next land on the dairy rung. Of the milk, yogurt, ice cream and cheese group, the department recommends two to three total servings. Finally, meat, poultry, fish, beans, eggs and nuts are given two to three recommended daily servings. With the addition of fatty, oil and sweet products, these groups make up the entire menu of consumable food items that you must daily sample from. But there is a definable characteristic for (nearly) all of them. To be consumed, they must die first.

This is quite obvious with animals, such as beef, poultry, fish or the like. But it is identical with (nearly) every other product. Peanuts are crushed and pulverized for peanut butter; grapes are annihilated for juice and jelly; tomatoes, basil and mushrooms face veggie genocide for Aunt Flora's famous spaghetti sauce. Although the chicken that laid the egg does not die, its early embryonic offspring (or another chicken) does. I am not attempting to turn all of my readers into vegans, but to point out a powerful phenomenon. The cycle of death continues for every single food product we place in our mouths and ingest in our stomachs – *except two.*

There are only two living organisms on this entire planet that are not destroyed when mankind consumes their product for food. Bees and cows. Milk is taken from the cow and the cow suffers no harm. Bees produce honey unscathed. As much sweet nectar as mankind consumes and as many milk mustaches line the faces of smiling children, the bee and the cow that produced it continue to live. Metaphorically, milk and honey are the only two "eternal" food products on the entire planet. For us to continue to exist, every other food product must die and be eliminated, except for bees and cows. "The land of enormous grapes" was inaccurate and lacking, as was my "land of endless gold and precious stones." Their inheritance was not a land overcrowded with bovine and stinging insects. It was a picture of a land that was meant to birth eternal life.

Now let me be abundantly clear, I did not say the land held eternal life. The inheritance God gave the Israelites was not the land; it was the law system that could reproduce the best possible outcome for humanity now living in a post-fall world. And the outcome of that law system had been designed so that it was to be a beacon of light to the rest of the world. As other nations continued to suffer under the effects of the fall, Israel was to stand out as healthier and more vibrant than any other nation, and so point other nations both to their law system, and to the God that lovingly had designed it. Remember Jesus' statements about being a city set on a hill? A lamp that never should be placed under a bushel? Israel, not just through its actions, but through its outcomes, was to broadcast to the rest of the world the God of Milk and Honey: the God of eternal life.

Let's look at honey one more time, just to clarify. We now realize that neither honey nor milk consumes their hosts, but the attributes of honey further the slogan. This is taken from the amazing facts page of the GoldenBlossomHoney.com website:

1. Honey never spoils. No need to refrigerate it. It can be stored unopened, indefinitely, at room temperature in a dry cupboard.

2. Honey is one of the oldest foods in existence. It was found in the tomb of King Tut and was still edible since honey <u>never spoils</u>.[1]

Honey, for all intents and purposes... is eternal. Or better yet, honey, if protected, isn't affected... *by the fall*.

It was the Promised Land, not just because it was promised to the Israelites. It was the Promised Land because it was also to contain God's pre-fall solutions for a post-fall world! And "Milk and Honey" was the marketing slogan to prove it. It was the only slogan God *could* have used. God wasn't just sending them into a good land geographically and agriculturally, but into a land in which they were to practice his "Milk and Honey" ordinances – and in so doing display the wondrous outcomes to the rest of the world.

We already discovered in the last chapter how that moniker was diluted, its power gelded. But as modern-day believers, it's time for us to recognize the purpose of His slogan and pick up the mantle.

1. http://goldenblossomhoney.com/education_facts.php

Chapter 5

THE MINISTRY OF "RECONCILIATION"

Ponder:
All this is from God, who reconciled us to himself through Christ and gave us the <u>ministry of reconciliation</u>: that God was reconciling the world to himself in Christ, not counting people's sins against them. And he has committed to us the message of reconciliation.
(2 Cor. 5:18-19, NIV, emphasis added)

This, then, is how you should pray: "Our Father in heaven, hallowed be your name, your kingdom come, your will be done, on earth as it is in heaven."
(Matt. 6:9-10, NIV)

Reconciliation is a term that predominantly has remained a religious distinction. The idea of a "ministry of reconciliation," under its common guise, refers to the bringing together of different people groups and societies to recognize past hurts and offenses. In addition, it often is mentioned in context of "reconciling" man back to God – or the redemption of man back to his Creator. But although these are crucial and critical parts of the Christian walk, the natural definition of the term exposes an even greater and deeper purpose.

Reconciliation is a *banking term.*

Remember that thing before Internet banking called a check register? It predominantly became extinct in our digital age. But back in the day, your checkbook contained a few pages of unfilled-out, gridded lines right at the front of the book. This was called a register. That register was supposed to be filled with all of your previous transactions: the money you had withdrawn from your account as well as the monetary deposits you had added. At the far right of the columns was a section entitled "total" where you would tally the "supposed" amount of money still left in your bank account at the time of the last withdrawal or deposit. I say "supposed" amount, because you couldn't be certain that the number in your register actually matched the correct amount of money stored at your bank. So you would contact your bank to get your official balance, in order to ensure that the amount written in your register matched the amount the bank actually held. If these two numbers matched, you were then said to have "reconciled" your account.

Let's break this down. There are two parts described above: the money that you personally calculated in your register and the money the bank actually held. So if the money in the bank was the real number, we could say that the amount in the bank was "perfect." It was the true and real amount of money you had acquired. Your register contained some derivation of that perfect number. When you finally matched up those two numbers, the derivation and the perfect merged.

This is the call of the Creator, and the prayer of Jesus in Matthew 6: To take the derivation in our current world and reconcile it back to the perfect. God is perfect in Spirit, Love and Truth, but mankind and existence, since the fall of man, are in the state of derivation. As man bows to the lure of sin, and suffers sin's intended biological, psychological, societal, generational and yes, spiritual outcomes, that derivation becomes a grosser and grosser distortion of the original. God's perfect plan is further disrupted and agitated and the intended prosperity and purpose of humanity is stagnated. But God's plan always has been the perfect, humanity and the world in its <u>pre-fall</u> state (before the sin of Adam): A time when existence was not marred by the combined strategies of sin and entropy. Despite the actuality of our post-fall world, the perfect remains the purpose.

This is the call to humanity: For His fallen creation to willingly embrace and actualize His intended pre-fall world. As man begins to create a world that more closely resembles its perfect intent and the perfect intent for mankind, he slowly is stepping toward God's desire of reconciliation. It begins with a personal reconciliation, to once again recognize and accept the One who made you and gave up His Son so that you could enter back into personal connection with your Creator. This is the call of evangelism, but "reconciliation" goes far deeper.

It's not just a personal invitation; it's a global call.

And the call is now made simple: Connect the derivation back to the perfect. And it is through seeing what is extinct in the perfect that displays what we must do in the derivation. For example, there is no disease in the perfect; therefore, we must do whatever we can to eliminate disease from the derivation. We can do this through more aggressive understanding and treatments of diseases, recognizing them as strategies and not merely unintended outcomes. We can recognize that the creator has crafted his vegetative and animal creation to help stave off diseases and complications, and begin to broadcast in more fervent ways the benefits of embracing less-processed food diets. We also can do so through real and documented healings.

There is no judgment in the perfect; so we can put down our moralistic bullhorns and love on each other simply as God's creation; despite ideological, religious and sexual orientations. There is no fear and destruction in the perfect, so we can begin to encourage and petition our media channels to more regularly broadcast the atrocities going on in other parts of the world, and we can come together with those of all faiths to attempt to alleviate the pain and suffering across the globe. There is no hate or selfish comparison in the perfect, so we consciously can chose to love and accept those that look, act and believe differently than we do.

There is no sin or its byproduct in the perfect, so we can begin to broadcast the *strategies of sin* to humanity and expose the enemy's purposeful intent. As I have already stated, entropy and sin are a byproduct of the fall. But sin is a choice; entropy is not. By distancing ourselves from the strategies of sin, we geld the power of entropy. The power comes in the understanding. And as you begin to grasp this understanding, you can begin to broadcast it to others. All the channels are in place; our world is now truly "flat." Our reach is global, our influence is unlimited.

SECTION 2: RESISTANCE

Chapter 6

THE DAMAGE OF "THE WAVE"

Ponder:
He who has an ear, let him hear....
(Rev. 2:7, NASB)

It started with an experiment... it grew into a potentially unstoppable movement... *and it ended in an instant.*

In the late 1960s, Ron Jones, a 10th-grade world history teacher living in the peaceful and germane suburbs of Palo Alto, Calif., nearly re-incubated one of the most genocidal regimes to ever govern on the face of this planet. At the beginning of a course study on Nazi Germany, a student posed a question to Jones and the rest of the class: "How could the German townspeople, railroad conductors, teachers, doctors, claim they knew nothing about the concentration camps and human carnage going on all around them?" The student's question reflected a common personal disbelief that any reasonable citizen would allow a regime capable of carrying out such atrocities to rise to power. Jones informed the student he didn't have the answer. It did, however, fuel Jones' desire to find out.

Jones decided the best way to discover the answer was through a quickly designed form of social experimentation. Under the guise of a new order of in-class behavior and conduct, Jones calculatedly infused control and nationalism into his daily teachings. Regimenting strict behavior and feeding his students community-pride rhetoric, within two days Jones surprisingly found he had commanded the full and unquestioning devotion of his students. It was a successful start. So Jones pushed deeper. His classroom behavior modification lessons lead to the birth of an in-class participatory program labeled "The Wave." Jones' students embraced the program with reckless and unquestioned abandon. His experiment now had a heartbeat.

The Wave escalated on campus. Students skipped other classes to sit in on Jones' daily Wave indoctrination exercises. The now-enlarged group of students readily conformed to the strict personal order and group pride of Jones' Wave orations. Within one week, more than 200 people enlisted in his "program," but by then it had already become a movement. The group designed a logo; produced banners; instigated a Wave salute; and donned Wave insignia-crested attire. The heartbeat of his movement now pulsated rapidly.

Non-Wave students were threatened and bullied into joining the growing rank-and-file masses. Jones' Wave students quickly were becoming a powerful army on campus. And the situation was getting out of control. The rebirth of something evil was being calculatedly launched on an unsuspecting suburban high school. *But Jones understood something about his propaganda that the students did not.* Despite the movement's apparent self-propulsion, it was *doomed for failure.* Jones knew how to end its foul heartbeat instantly: All it would take was the exposure of its leader.

On Friday of that week, Jones announced to his steadily growing Wave army that his weeklong experiment actually was a test for admission into the nationwide Wave movement rising up in communities across the country. He commanded that his students assemble after school in the gymnasium for the first Wave national telecast. The students were informed that the national Wave director would address all the sprouting chapters across the country. Full Wave attire was required. The students unquestioningly complied.

Wearing Wave armbands and sporting Wave banners, more than 200 students waited intently, sitting at full attention. This day, there was no usual casual teen conversation, no restless movement. All eyes stared forward toward the large blank projection screen that would, at any moment, broadcast a powerful speech to rally the students to further action.

But the screen remained blank.

No leader materialized; no powerful speech was heard. As the minutes ticked by, the students grew uncomfortable. Then, after what seemed like hours of chilling silence, Jones grabbed the microphone. Looking over the congregated assembly, he boldly announced there was no national Wave leader; there were no other Wave chapters. There was dead silence in the room, as if the students awaited Jones to continue and somehow negate his last statement – but Mr. Jones remained silent.

Slowly, the reality of his statement began to prick at the souls of his disaffected students. They felt betrayed, wrestling with the powerful dynamics of the prior week's events. What they had become a part of felt so powerful. It had given the students a sense of identity and brought an entire young community together. Before, they were a regimented army. Now, it seemed they were without a cause, but still infused with a desire to continue on course.

That was the result Jones was looking for.

Jones wheeled a small television to the center of the stage. With all sternness and compassion, he looked over his student army and stated, "This is the leader you have been following."

With a click of a knob the small screen hissed into focus. This screen did show a leader in the midst of a speech to his movement. That leader was Adolf Hitler. The speech was the Nuremburg Address. As Hitler's frenzied speech continued and his gathered mob shouted back their unmitigated support, Jones' students quickly grasped the correlation. They were wearing armbands. They held banners. They greeted each other with a similar salute. They also would have done anything for their leader. They just didn't know whom they had been ultimately following. *But now they knew.* From that day on, there was no more desire for a Wave movement. It was never mentioned, never re-instigated. The movement's seemingly unstoppable power was instantly annihilated – at the exposure of its annihilative leader.

Mankind has been dropped into the middle of a massive Wave movement. It seems so right, so natural and so conducive of how we are to act. And it is strategically ingrained into every facet of society. It, too, seems unstoppable. But it also can end in a moment. I believe all it will take is the exposure of its leader…

Chapter 7

DISSECTING BARABBAS: RELEASING A MURDERER AMONG US:

Ponder:
So when the crowd had gathered, Pilate asked them, "Which one do you want me to release to you: Jesus Barabbas, or Jesus who is called the Messiah?... "Barabbas," they answered.
(Matt. 27:17-21, NIV)

Even if your only experience with church is the occasional Easter or Good Friday service, chances are you have heard the story of Barabbas. Although the Bible gives us little backstory on the man, he played an essential role in the rejection of Jesus and Christ's ultimate crucifixion. The story unfolds in Matthew 26-27. The Roman prefect Pilate – finding no true fault in the person of Jesus and not wishing to become the scapegoat in the death of an "innocent" man – offers the turbulent crowd two options. The crowd could either release the now-bloodied and disfigured Jesus, who Pilate believed had suffered commensurately for his "crimes," or emancipate Barabbas, a known murderer and thief currently incarcerated under Caesar's governmental control.

Either way, Pilate was to wash his hands of the matter. The choice and responsibility now lay in the hands of the people. And they chose Barabbas. But Barabbas' release, though the volitional and personal decision of the crowd, had nothing to do with concern for Barabbas' well-being. Barabbas' freedom merely ensured Jesus' elimination. Because Pilate's offer to the crowd was volitional and personal, Barabbas became a means to an end.

There is a well-captured moment in Mel Gibson's movie *The Passion of the Christ* that displays this tension. During the trial scene, the now-released Barabbas passes directly in front of the High Priest Caiaphas, the man shouting the loudest for Barabbas' release. As the two men brush shoulders, there is a forced moment of acknowledgement. Caiaphas' face grossly displays the disdain he holds for Barabbas. To Caiaphas, Barabbas is of no value. Barabbas merely serves as the conduit to eliminate the dissident that had been diverting and converting much of the High Priest's former flock. As the two men pass out of view, attention shifts back to the now-condemned Christ. We never see or hear of Barabbas again.

But this particular historical moment did not exist in a vacuum. And by dissecting the very few bits of information we are given about Barabbas and unlocking his untold story, I will illuminate the ultimate enemy of mankind; uncloak his objective patterns of destruction; unlock where mankind has partnered with these patterns; expose the church's tragic failure; and provide the precise area for repentance and regeneration. The path toward those discoveries begins where the Bible leaves off. It begins with Barabbas' release.

UNINTENDED CONSEQUENCE

When the angry mob chooses Barabbas over Jesus, the story doesn't end for Barabbas, or for those shouting for the murderer's emancipation. The mob's decision discharges a host of new and potentially catastrophic possibilities. But the mob itself has no say in these new contingencies. From that moment on, the future is no longer theirs to control. They had granted this man Barabbas far more freedom than they could have imagined. Though the religious leaders and the mob thought they were simply ensuring the crucifixion of the One they so vehemently despised, in actually they were sanctioning the possibility for their own death.

Releasing a murderer meant that eventually that man might choose to murder you.

"Give us Barabbas," was actually the unwitting declaration of, "Free the man who may someday murder us." The mob's decision was final. They had chosen the execution of the Christ. But the consequences of that decision were just beginning. After the riot had ended, and the darkness of night rested over the three crosses on the hill of the skull, the mob had successfully crucified their rival, and *released a murderer into their community.* Though they had shouted, "Let Jesus' blood be on our hands and children," it is doubtful that either the mob or the religious leaders had the foresight to see the consequences of that proclamation. In the elimination of one, they had gained the other. If any of those who had shouted for Barabbas' release were to wake up the next morning and find their children murdered, their wives brutally raped and all their financial security stolen away, there would be no one to blame but themselves.

There was now a killer running loose in their community. And they'd been the ones to release him.

But the mob's decision extended far beyond merely those gathered at the trial. With his release, the entire human landscape became his potential prey. The phrase, "Give us Barabbas," – if Barabbas was endlessly crafty and cunning enough – had the capacity to translate to, "Kill us all." Of course it is highly unlikely that one man could eliminate an entire population. And although this scenario is highly implausible, theoretically, *it is possible.* But metaphorically, I believe the Holy Spirit was uncovering something far more diabolical and objective.

A FAR BIGGER – AND MORE RELEVANT – STORY

It is possible that much more is being disclosed here than just the unwritten story of a lone murderer running loose in Jerusalem after the death of Christ. Over the context of the four Gospels, we are given three key characteristics of the man Barabbas. He is referred to as a robber (John 18:40, NASB), a murderer and an insurrectionist (Mark 15:7, Luke 23:19). If we translate insurrection as the desire to overthrow and/or cause violent destruction of an authority, Barabbas' three main motivating drivers were to "steal, kill and destroy." Does this sound familiar? It should.

> *The thief (Satan) comes only to steal and kill and destroy; I have come that they may have life, and have it to the full.* (John 10:10, NIV, parenthesis mine)

Barabbas was just a man. But his three characteristics uncover what the man represents: an ultimate spiritual enemy with a single collective goal of killing, stealing and destroying humankind, or those made in the image of his ultimate enemy. And just like releasing the man Barabbas, with the rejection of the One (Christ) we are granting authority to the other. Jesus claimed He was the only way. But he verified His statement and exposed the danger of His rejection in the story of Barabbas. Rejecting the Christ does not give man the option to go his own way, to seek a different path toward the same ultimate Truth. There are, and have always been, two paths. And the path "more traveled," the path that rejects Christ, comes with a powerful price tag. Just like the gathered mob shouting for Christ's death, the consequences to rejecting God are once again outside of man's control. But the potential for destruction is far, far greater.

Barabbas, the man, may have never killed again. Other things may have chosen to occupy his time after his release. But we, as self-sufficient humanity with no need of Christ, have released an ultimate murderer into our midst with no other agenda *but* destruction. And his evidence is all around us if we have the eyes to see clearly. Ask the mother who must I.D. her 17-year-old daughter's dead corpse after a heroin overdose, or the tens of millions of children dying of AIDS in Africa, or the one in four women who has been raped or sexually assaulted in America, or the gaunt inner-city family members barely able to afford enough to eat a single meal a day. The list goes on and on, if we are really paying attention. While a minute portion of the world appears to be living free and easy, the rest of humanity has been ransacked and decimated by the ultimate Barabbas that has long since been released. Rejection of the one granted authority to the other. And his authority manifests through mankind's demise. Just like the mob having released the original Barabbas, we have no one to blame but ourselves.

A QUESTION TO PONDER

Is this correlation between the two Barabbases too great a stretch? Am I grasping at straws in order to prove my own allegorical point? To answer those questions requires us to step back into the original story. How might the man Barabbas have gotten away with recurrent murder after his release? If your ultimate desire is unabated bloodlust, would you annihilate society's most influential, wealthiest and publicly known? Certainly not. By attacking the social elite and well respected, you guarantee a quicker capture. Investigations would ensue, curfews would be imposed, social militias would be formed – all bent on your exposure, incarceration and ultimate annihilation. Why? Because you attacked those society cared the most about.

But if you attacked and destroyed the nominal, the unloved and the outcasts, who would call for an investigation? As long as you kept yourself hidden, predominantly attacked the fringe of society, and maintained some control over your pathology, your murderous rampage could continue and perpetuate. Sadly, many might even claim you were doing these rejected and nominal people – and people groups – a favor by eliminating them.

CARRYING ON "DADDY'S" TRAITS

As barbaric and cold as that idea appears, it uncovers exactly how the ultimate Barabbas garners assistance in his unflinching agenda of man's destruction. Consider the language used by some anti-homosexual groups when describing the "providential purpose" of the mass viral executioner, AIDS. Or the racist, hateful sentiment bellowed out by a portion of America's citizenry during the years of segregation. Or perhaps reflect on the vehement and deadly language used by Hutus in regard to the Tutsis in Rwanda, or the Shiites toward the Sunnis, the Muslims toward the Zionists, etc., etc., ad infinitum. Instead of recognizing the ultimate Barabbas running loose in our midst, portions of humanity justify, herald and even commit the enemy's agenda for him. We have not only released Barabbas, we also personally manifest him whenever we act against another human being with disgust, hatred or enmity.

Scripture appears to back up the last claim. For there is one other bit of specific information we are given about the man, Barabbas: his name. It is constructed through the fusing of two Greek words: "bar" meaning "son of" and "abba" meaning "father." Barabbas, in Greek, translates to "son of a father." The name is highly nebulous, until we look back at Barabbas' three characteristics. Suppose a star college quarterback grows up and has three sons. One devotes his time to painting, another to tinkering with old muscle cars. But the final son starts pee-wee football at the age of eight, and by his sophomore year of high school is already the starting quarterback for the varsity team. Which son would most people state is "just like his old man?" The son who displayed the same characteristics as his father. So then, based on his characteristics, Barabbas might be described as "son of destruction."

The term "Barabbas" carries serious generational weight. It offers the hearer no information except its purposed reference to the continuation of a lineage. I believe it is through the characteristics of the son that man is exposed as a grandson or granddaughter in that lineage. In other words, by unwittingly partnering with Barabbas, we perpetuate a generational transfer of destruction. Sometimes that destruction is self-inflicted. Consider the millions suffering from venereal diseases and AIDS in America; the destructive results of skyrocketing meth and prescriptive medicine addiction among our teenagers; or the lives of individuals and families decimated from debilitating credit card debt. Sometimes that destruction is residual. The children born with dramatic birth defects after a corporation poisons the local water supply with its hazardous waste; the millions kidnapped and raped around the world through human trafficking to support humanity's degrading sexual preferences; the millions dead or dying from cigarettes or second-hand smoke; the entire displaced inner-city neighborhood left on the street after a real-estate developer acquires the land for "urban renewal." At other times, destruction starts ideologically and manifests existentially. Consider the 50 million unborn babies aborted in just a few decades; the countless hundreds of thousands left with devastated lives, families and work environments after gambling casinos propagated on reservations or riverfronts; or the high percentage of marriages ripped apart after society determined that the "freedom of pornography" was a healthy commercial enterprise.

I make no claims of moral imposition here; I am merely pointing out that the byproduct of each of these examples produces objective and calculable destruction across numerous realms of existence (physical, social, economical, psychological, generational, etc.) We can rationalize and spin our marketing to accentuate the positives of many of these actions, but we can't erase the statistical facts of their outcomes.

A question then arises: Is mankind's ultimate intent its own, or even another's, destruction?

Certainly not, but destruction is our lot because the majority of the world inadvertently shouted, "Give us Barabbas!" when it rejected Christ. But the blame for Barabbas' release and unchallenged genocidal pillaging does not simply fall to those having rejected Christ. It also falls to those claiming to have chosen him. Man has not rejected the true Christ; he has rejected what some portions of the church made Christ out to be. The world appears to have distanced itself from the *true* Christ, because the world seems to want little to do with the Christ that some of the church presents. And sadly, in many areas of Barabbas' destruction, such as divorce, drug usage and STDs, the church either mimics or surpasses the national average percentages. Based on the evidence, we, as the church, have also not only said, "Give us Barabbas;" we appear to have given in to him and then attack others for doing the same.

Tragically, this has led to a culture that now shifts the blame of society's woes toward *those that follow Christ*. The culture protects opportunities to destroy itself, while embargoing Christians from bringing illumination to the destructive patterns and providing healing.

As true Christians, we must now shout, "Give us the Christ!" But we must shout this to ourselves, not just to the rest of humanity. To the rest of humanity we must be unadulterated love in a dark world we've helped create. We must be actions, not just words. And our first words must be that of apology, not simply apologetics. We must give back the true Christ to a humanity that prefers Barabbas due, in part, to our moments of hypocrisy. It's time to understand that the unwritten story of the man Barabbas is the very real story of mankind today.

There is now a killer running loose in our community. And, if we're honest, we've helped to release him.

WHAT WE MUST DO

The first step is to recognize where we have partnered with Barabbas in our own lives, and then in our corporate bodies. We must focus on the byproduct of destruction, and then search it out. Barabbas is a multi-headed hydra, well cloaked in many areas. Many of those areas we rationalize and even sanction through our supposed "piety." But using a baseline of "destruction," his evidence exposes him – and us. We must recognize this destruction as it pertains to all of humanity. As you have already discovered, Christianity transcends its religious confines, and the church must communicate on a level that is clear and objective to all, regardless of the audience's ideology, religious affiliation or cultural background.

Which leads to the second step. We must make a verbal declaration of, "Give us the Christ!" and then live according to His revelation and principles. We can't simply tell people about His principles, or condemn others for not adhering to them; *we must live them.* If we choose and embrace the true Christ, the evidence of our lives will be so winsome and transformative that others will inquire of us. Remember, Jesus Christ said, "Be prepared to give an account for the joy inside of you." Aware or not, the world is desperately counting on a church that makes a difference and alleviates Barabbas' aftermath. It doesn't care which denomination or denominations it comes from.

Chapter 8

LIBERATION OF THE BODY-SNATCHED

Ponder:
For our struggle is not against flesh and blood, but against the rulers,
against the authorities, against the powers of this dark world and against
the spiritual forces of evil in the heavenly realms.
(Eph. 6:12, NIV)

"Hate the sin, but love the sinner." The preceding phrase, quoted by many Christians, is a nice idiom, but it is definitely difficult to put into practice. After all, the individual is the one engaged in sin – to disconnect the sinner from the sin requires Herculean effort, especially when the "sin" is one most churchgoers might find physically repulsive. (I'll leave you to guess which sins that might refer to.) But there is a different lens through which to look at the connection between sin and sinner. Through this lens the demarcation line becomes crystal clear. To begin to focus this lens I will first use scripture, and then I will use pop-science fiction. And I'll wager that the more relevant and relatable understanding of the Kingdom-minded relationship between "sin and sinner" will come from Hollywood.

In the scriptures, the Apostle Paul asserts that the church's battle is not against flesh and blood, but against principalities and powers. Author Greg Boyd crafted a very easy formula to simplify this passage: *"If it has flesh and blood, it is not your enemy."* Much of the church – including myself at times – forgets that all of humanity is made in the image of God as Genesis 1 asserts. Each human on this planet, no matter how debase, immoral, violent or arrogant his or her actions might be, still bears the glorious image of God. The most adamant member of the ACLU, the most ardent devil worshiper, the loudest gay-rights activist – all bear the glorious image of God. When the church began to distance itself from this reality and (more tragically) commit actions against this truth, the chasm between the world and the church began to widen. As righteous soldiers, the church went to war. But we forgot who our enemy was, turning our sights on others bearing God's image, instead of remaining focused on principalities and powers as Paul mandated. But this is somewhat understandable:

> *Where there is no revelation, people cast off restraint....*" (Prov. 29:18, NIV)

Though this passage is most often quoted using the unsaved world as the "people" of the verse, the unrestrained today also can be the church. When we lost the revelation of who (or what) our enemy was, our attacks grew unrestrained on those we determined were operating outside God's holy standard. Without a tangible peg to hang up the appropriate picture of the "sin and sinner" connection, we began to make our own judgments. And in doing so, both sides have cast off restraint: the church in its vehement attack of "sinners," and the world in its unrestrained embrace of "sin." My hope is now to provide a tangible revelation through a very unlikely source.

REVELATION AND INSIGHT THROUGH POP CULTURE

In the past 40 to 50 years there have been numerous science fiction films featuring "body-snatching" aliens. The main plot line of these diverse film offerings is that some "force" has entered a community, city, state or nation and has begun "snatching" the bodies of the region's inhabitants. The force does so (although its method widely varies from film to film) by connecting itself to the physical body of its human container, turning the two into one flesh. The infected human now becomes a carrier of the agenda of the force that snatched it. Slowly, this force travels throughout the locale, snatching as many as it can, and turning them all to like mind.

Inevitably in these films, we find a hero. The hero is one who has not been yet snatched by the force. Instead he or she watches as friends, neighbors and the entire community come under the power and coercion of this force. The snatched, now totally under the control of the coercive power, become ambassadors for the new force, asserting to those not yet under control (including the hero), "It's wonderful here, we're happier than we've even been, come join us." And yet surprisingly, despite their peaceful-faced petitions, the hero never accepts the invitation to join the rest of his snatched community. Why not? After all, the snatched appear peaceful and content, claiming to finally be in a far better place. But the hero recognizes the coerced state of his or her fellow community. The hero won't let the claims of the snatchers replace his or her love for the value and importance of the snatched. Instead, he or she goes to war.

But how does the hero go to war? He goes to war for the snatched – and against the snatchers. But herein lies the dilemma: At the moment of battle, the snatched and the snatcher are one and the same. His enemy is not the snatched, for the snatched is his neighbor, relative, friend, coworker, or fellow community member. So he must protect the snatched... solely by destroying and removing the snatcher. He cannot heed the "coerced" petitions of the snatched. His love for the people who have been snatched cannot trump the supposedly genuine pleadings of the snatcher inside them. He cannot harm or attack them, for they and he are the same.

Even if the hero is the only one left in the battle, he or she doesn't stop until all under the spell of the snatchers are free, no matter how hard they fight against him or her, or claim their unabashed allegiance to the snatchers.

BACK TO THE BIBLE

We often look at "sinners" from a moralistic perspective, in other words, we tend to judge from a "God said it, I believe it, and therefore you also must obey it" mindset. We have created ministries and even lobbyist groups around this idea. But in doing so, we are by very nature associating these individuals with their snatchers if and when they fail. And in response to this, Jesus said why should we try to remove the speck from our brother's eye when we have a log in our own. Instead, we should look beyond just the morality of sin to its dangerous and deadly consequences. For these consequences attack the "sinner" despite his or her vehement petitions to the contrary. To the snatched, then, we point out the damaging consequences of actions, but aim all our force of attack on the snatcher and his cadre.

And that is who we battle for: men, women, fathers, husbands, mothers, teachers, workmates, students, children, it's an endless list. The battle isn't just a spiritual one; it's also a physical one. The destruction of the snatched is found in the damaging aftereffects of humanity's own actions. Just as we once did, society gives itself to dangerous and physically damaging pleasures, without considering the cost. And now we have the disease, destruction, depression and divorce to prove it. Humanity now suffers under outcomes that are merely the enemy's intent of our self-oriented actions. Because of the immediate hurt and damage that is ubiquitous in our society, our love for the snatched must not just be for their souls, but their bodies and minds as well.

Once they are free, those who had been snatched are permanently and volitionally indebted to the hero. But until that moment, they'll fight the hero with every resource necessary to continue the snatcher's agenda.

The hero can only bring about liberation if he or she is free of the snatchers. Only then are they free to battle for the snatched. Otherwise, the battle is against the snatched and for the snatcher, for doing nothing for the snatched gives concession for the snatcher to bind people at will. There can be no victorious battle, until the hero is free first. This is why we can't claim to be the "moralistic" heroes in this battle. Because we were just as snatched. For some reason we seem to forget our former nature when we become saved. We attack others for the very things we used to practice, and wonder why we make little cultural impact.

Instead of attacking others who are just as snatched as we used to be, we must point humanity to the ultimate hero, the One who was never corrupted by the snatchers. It is only He that has any right to command the release of the snatcher, and proclaim victory for the snatched. Jesus, as the ultimate hero, allows us to make the bold but absolutely true declaration that he whom the Son sets free is free indeed. It is only because of His freedom, that we have not the "right" – but the mandate – to be His humble heroes, in His name.

And we must not add piety and moralistic sympathy to the reasoning behind our feelings toward the snatched. Remember, we're not the heroes. We've merely been set free by the ultimate hero, and He has taught us, somewhat unknowingly, how He battles for us. Ask the risen Lord to teach you how to battle for the snatched and against the snatcher, and watch the ultimate Hero set people free like never before.

Chapter 9

UNDERSTANDING SIN'S "WAGE"

Ponder:
"For the wages of sin...."
(Rom. 6:23, NIV)

Romans 6:23 is another verse commonly used in church evangelism. But to really grasp its full objectivity, we need to expand this scripture to its logical conclusion, adding the words that are not evident but assumed. From an employee/employer context, this passage isn't simply referring to the "wages of sin," but the wages of the *vocation* of sin. Using the analogy of business, we now can get *strategic*. There are at least 23 million people in the United States currently looking for employment. And while a particular vocation or a specific corporation is itself important when considering one's next career path, the potential salary is often more determining.

Imagine a future employer telling you that the position you had always dreamed of was now yours – but that the salary provided would not support your current car payment(s), house mortgage/rent, or food bills, expenses critical to the survival of yourself and your family. Would you be willing to take the position? Naturally, you would take into account the salary and compensation package before making any vocational decision, would you not? For many, the job requirements and opportunities are far less important than that all-too-necessary wage. And yet when it comes to the vocation of sin, most of us do the exact opposite.

There are many that choose to reject God and his laws because He... *doesn't let humanity have any fun.* God is a squelcher of pleasure and those that reject him are blissfully unfettered, able to engage in their own self-oriented pleasures, free from religion's condemnation and guilt. It is the Bible that calls many of man's supposed pleasures sins, so by rejecting God one can also reject His definition.

So using the verse at the beginning of this chapter, let's create a hypothetical business for a second. I will refer to this business entity as "Sin Unlimited." Now for those having rejected God's definition of the word, this would be nothing more than a company of unrestrictive pleasure. Sounds like a pretty good deal. But that's just the work requirement; it's not the salary or compensation package. What lucrative compensation carrot is dangled in front of the potential employee of Sin Unlimited to get them to jump at the position?

For the wages (or compensation) of (the vocation of) sin is death.

Wow. So the salary affixed to the position at Sin Unlimited is your ultimate destruction. It is simply the compensation package bestowed upon the employed. The *job requirement* is engagement in sin. But "pleasure" is not the salary benefit of the position – *death is*. Here lies the inevitable, because in any vocation, the salary comes attached to the position. The employer is obligated to deliver the compensation to his or her employee; it is mandatory, regardless of whether the employee was aware of the compensation package. So then employment at Sin Unlimited must appear to be a highly desirable and sought-after position, so that the next logical question is never asked: "OK, I like the position, but what is the compensation package?"

This is where the fantasy world of marketing and media is channeled. Media portrays a world in which the vocation of sinful pleasure is up-played, but the salary is rarely mentioned or even considered (unless it equates to a plot point in the story). The secular agenda, in its deliberate attempt to remove the dogmatism of supposedly pleasure-shackling mandates of the God of the Bible, attempts to glorify sin's "pleasure."

But this only further binds mankind, for the salary package is commensurate with the job description. While secular media becomes the recruiter for additional employees at Sin Unlimited, it is not its ultimate board of directors. They also are subjected to the compensation package of the vocation. But marketing and media work effectively well as recruiters because their fictitious world portrayals repeatedly show the individual so blissfully engaging in the vocation that the salary question is never asked – until its too late. Fictitious media and advertising inadvertently recruit for new employees, and the news agencies broadcast *the tragic results of those who have garnered the salaries.*

If we want hell, then hell is what we'll have. (Jack Johnson, "Cookie Jar")

Perhaps the best example of the false glorification of the position, while also forced to experience the compensation package, would be the pornographic industry. Although in their films, their "characters" engage in free and repeated promiscuous sex without consequence, the actors and actresses off-stage suffer the cataclysmic repercussions of the reality of their actions. Many stars in the porn industry barely revel in their glory, for though in their films unprotected sex is far more enticing to the audience and lucrative to the studios, the consequences are the death of many through AIDS and other biological diseases and psychological complications.

Despite the aggressive work ethic of those employed at Sin Unlimited, there is no advancement, for the salary works against the employee. Better yet, the salary is specifically designed to eradicate the one receiving it. The corporation is always suffering employee loss. So for the corporation to continue, new employees must replace those that have built up enough "savings" of death that death eventually overtakes them. It is an endless cycle – as long as no one asks the salary question.

God revealed in scripture what we now see in the lives of those around us, what is plastered in our newspaper headlines and what takes up a growing portion of our news segments. Primetime and cable television glamorize the job position at Sin Incorporated. News networks and statisticians document the wage. The world is full of people suffering under the crushing weight of a salary they never bargained for. Instead of blaming them for their employ, we need to bandage their wounds. And we must broadcast from the rooftops the reality of Sin Incorporated's compensation package.

Remember: sin doesn't merely have the possibility of leading to death; it is its ultimate goal. So why doesn't everyone receive the ultimate salary (death) when engaging in sin's pleasures? The answer is found the next chapter.

Chapter 10

TROUBLE IN PARADISE: THE DANGER OF "MATURING" SIN

Ponder:
"… and sin, when it is full- grown, leads to death."
(James 1:15, NIV)

Although scripture asserts that the wages of sin "is death," many people appear to get off scott free. We certainly see much of our society engaging in 'sinful' behaviors, only to blissfully meander through life supposedly unscathed. Sure, you can harbor the self-righteous hope that they'll get theirs in the end, but is that any way to see another person made in God's image? Yet as a believer, practicing restraint from many of society's greatest pleasures, have you ever wondered, "What gives?" Solomon struggled with this many millennia ago, but what about today? We've sanctioned many sinful behaviors, actions that are now governmentally legal, but are still not approved by God and His mandates. Is the concept of sin growing irrelevant if those engaging in it never seem to experience sin's wage? To answer that question, I will ask a different question.

Would you say that a two-year-old child, although a living member of mankind, has reached his or her full human potential? Of course not. A two-year-old constantly is maturing into what he or she was designed to eventually become. But the baby does not stay two forever. Now let's suppose that you are a rather fit individual with an above-average amount of strength. Though the two-year-old may grow up to be a 325-pound NFL linebacker at maturity, is it highly probable that at the age of two you would still be able to control that child? Certainly you would. Even as this individual reached the beginning of the teen years it still is likely that your personal fortitude and strength could subdue the young fledgling of a man. Now how about during his early college years, when he has reached 260 pounds, eats 9,000 calories a day, runs the 40-yard dash in 4.4 seconds and curls dumbbells weighing more than 100 pounds?

So what happened? How did the little child who was so easily subdued suddenly become the behemoth capable of rendering indescribable pain on your fit torso? The child went through the natural process of maturity, and during that process gained strength, size and stamina. Eventually this child *overthrew your ability to control him*. In the same way, sin masquerades as a little infant, easily controllable by its adopter. Notice the control that secular humanism appears to warrant over sinful pleasure:

> *Short of harming others or compelling them to do likewise, individuals should be permitted to express their sexual proclivities and pursue their life-styles <u>as they desire</u>. (Humanist Manifesto II, emphasis added)*

But as sin is embraced it begins to grow into its mature state: death. As sin continues to mature, it becomes less and less controllable, and eventually the action no longer even resembles pleasure. Hollywood often portrays these downward spirals in films such as *Blow, Traffic, Less than Zero, Leaving Las Vegas, When a Man Loves a Woman*, and countless others, while never grasping that the end result of death, addiction and misery is not some disconnected outcome *but the intent*. Addiction in any form becomes merely a required motion that does not produce pleasure but instead momentarily anesthetizes the pain that has been produced because of the action itself. But just as without warning one day the two-year-old baby becomes the linebacker with strength enough to subdue you, so mankind does not control at what moment sin matures into death, or addiction, as you will soon discover in the next chapter.

But death doesn't have to be so final here, little deaths can occur from the first time one engages in sin, such as the death of brain mass through drug usage, the death of self respect after a desired sexual encounter turns south, the death of a family relationship when daddy chooses one quick and hidden night of passion on a business trip, the death self control as nicotine overtakes the curious smoker, the list goes on and on. Death occurs whether we are aware of it or not. Ultimate death is the full maturity of sin, but like our linebacker, even as a young man in college or even late high school it is likely that he could still overtake you in a fight, even if he hasn't reached full maturity. And when sin matures, its consequences are often far more devastating than just the death of the individual involved. Let me give a hypothetical scenario.

TROUBLE IN PARADISE

Suppose a particular resort chain were to focus its media marketing predominantly on its free spiritedness toward sexual behavior and expression. By choosing to globally market in such a manner, these resorts would no doubt flourish with throngs of sexually promiscuous and pleasure-centered individuals. That is the demographic they chose as their core target audience. With its profitable demographic secured, the resort would encourage freedom of sexuality through its events, games and nightlife.

But let's say a finding were to surface that during the last five years 30% of those having contracted AIDS in the U.S. had visited this particular resort chain, and of that cohort, although having numerous partners prior to and after their resort visit, 75% had contracted the disease only after their visits? Perhaps the study began to pick up some media steam, and a large weekly global magazine decided to publish an article describing these findings under a headline reading, "AIDS Resort?"

Now, the hotel staff and management and its corporate executives could attempt to distance themselves from any blame, citing a strict "safer sex" policy and providing a steady supply of condoms in every resort bedroom. But after a story such as this floods the national and international media, what happens to the tourism numbers at the resort? Moreover, the resort has been indelibly branded with a label that its PR team can't fully wear off. Even if the resort choses to redirect its marketing toward wholesome family fun, could the resort fully shake its inflicting and detrimental moniker?

Free-spirited sexuality was the quick and immediate marketing draw. But objective and immutable biological destruction from a maturing sinful behavior became the catalyst to the resort's (and its patrons) demise. Moreover, those employed at the resort would also suffer serious recourse, for there would be no more jobs if there were no more resort. It is also likely that the employees would find new employment a difficult proposition, for what other local establishment would hire these past employees, knowing that their own customer base might be highly offended to learn that their ten year old's arts and crafts class lesson was being conducted by the former activities director at "AIDS Resort?" So the potential overall and continual damage for the previous employees is staggering, the parent corporation has suffered major losses, and numerous former guests are permanent patrons of AIDS clinics, hospitals and morgues, all because of the "sinful" money making decision of the corporation's executive team.

This says nothing about the innocent townspeople in the resort area, having fed and raised their families on the money collected from selling their wares to resort patrons. What do you suppose happens to them and their desire to live prosperous and peaceful lives? Where does our humanist quote fit in now?

"Short of harming others or compelling them to do likewise, individuals should be permitted to express their sexual proclivities and pursue their life-styles as they desire."
(Humanist Manifesto II, emphasis added)

Despite claims, or even desires, to the contrary, harm was brought to others. Not simply through their intentional actions, but through the unintended outcomes. The preceding was a hypothetical scenario, but its reality transpires all around us. Spend time with a doctor, a psychologist, a police officer and the like and you will hear story upon story of the effects of outcomes that vastly surpass the benefits of their initial actions.

Does this take away from the spiritual side of sin's damage? Absolutely not, but it helps us more fully understand God's love and compassion for His greatest creation, humanity. We see His love, not in the restriction of actions but in His liberation from outcomes (read Deuteronomy 28 in this light). God desires that none should perish, not just spiritually, but in all aspects of their lives, both here on this earth and in the life (or death) to come.

Sin masquerades as an infant, only to decimate and destroy when it reaches its intended maturity. We haven't made much headway by berating people for playing with the infant. Perhaps it is time to start lovingly observing, illuminating and addressing sin in its mature state.

In the next chapter we discover just how overthrowing maturing sin becomes.

Chapter 11

THE INSANITY OF ADDICTION

Ponder:
All flesh is grass, and all its loveliness is like the flower of the field. The grass withers, the flower fades… surely the people are grass. The grass withers, the flower fades….
(Is. 40:6-8, NASB)

The television show *Intervention* allows the viewing public to peer into the troubled life of an addict. Each show brings together family, friends and coworkers in a last-ditch attempt to rescue a loved one from the damaging grip of addiction. By gathering the addict's family and friends together in a single room, the addicted can recognize the huge panorama of love and concern surrounding them. But even more importantly, the addict comes face to face with all of those who have been negatively affected by his or her personal choices of action. Addiction is often less about the individual and far more about the affected surrounding society and environment.

One of the common petitions at an intervention is the retelling of the definition of insanity: "Doing the same thing over again but expecting a different result."

It is the assurance that whatever physical, psychological or emotional utopia the addicted individual wished to achieve, it is only a mirage, slipping further and further away with each repeated use or action. C.S. Lewis coins this addictive cycle in his book "The Screwtape Letters" as, "the law of diminishing returns." But hidden inside this definition of insanity lies a profound fallacy: The addicted individual, who once was healthy, <u>was</u> doing the same thing over and over again – but at the first moment of addiction *a different result occurred.*

We tend to compartmentalize individuals. An afternoon network television program that spotlights pornographic addiction, for example, might detail the tragic lives of a few addicted men, citing alarming statistics such as the rise in child molestation cases, rapes and the like.

Yet in typical "fair and balanced" fashion, the program also might feature a psychologist or sex therapist bestowing the liberating value of pornography when used in a "healthy" manner. The show might even include a husband and wife blissfully retelling how watching erotic videos saved their sex lives and possibly their marriage. The addicted and the healthy are compartmentalized. The tragic outcome of addiction is not the fault of the pornography, or the gambling, or the drinking; instead it is the fault of the individual unable to control himself, and/or experience the beneficial and "healthy" features of these actions. This is why alcohol ads now state: "drink *responsibly.*"

But no one sitting in a bar on a Saturday night walks in the front door thinking, "Tonight's my night to get addicted." No one who gets on the computer to periodically look at porn clicks to the first website and says, "I hope this enslaves me tonight." No one who routinely plays blackjack with his or her friends on Monday evenings and watches World Championship Poker on satellite TV thinks, "Tonight gambling will start destroying my life." They simply continue doing the same thing they had done in the past. And yet, at the point of addiction, a different result occurs.

Surprisingly, the difference at the moment of addiction has little to do with the individual. It is far more tied to the individual's physical body (or flesh). While an individual may claim, "I have needs," in actually it is the body that has needs. The body is, in essence, its own autonomous entity. It operates independently of your own will. The breaths you take, the blood that pumps, the electricity that shoots through your brain as you read this, all are taking place outside of your personal control. But the body initially requires the man's will to fill its own selfish needs. Once the will of the man has gone down that path, the physical body begins to take over.

And at the point of addiction, the will of the man has been completely hijacked by the physical body of the man.

But now we can uncover that the process to domination, the pathway to addiction, is simply continuing in the same course of action over and over again. It's not a battle of the will. It is a battle of the flesh (the physical body).

The first instance of addiction is very much like the moment a gun finally goes off in a game of Russian roulette. The more times one plays, the greater the probability the gun will discharge. It is the repetition of addiction-producing actions that provide the bullets that fill the gun's empty chambers. But in this metaphor we discover the danger. For while the potentially addicted individual may be the one holding the gun, the gun itself is the flesh (physical body) of the individual.

In other words, the individual (the will) does not determine when the gun goes off; his physical body does.

So the individual who repeatedly pulls the trigger – only to have the gun continually misfire – naively concludes, "I'm in control here." In reality, bullets are being added to the gun without the individual being the least bit aware. The gun goes off when the flesh, not the will, decides it's time to fire. All the individual can do prior to the moment of addictive discharge is walk away from the gun. He cannot begin the game and control the result.

Unfortunately, leaving the table – even prior to addiction – is harder than one might think.

Keeping with the Russian roulette metaphor, neuroscience and genetics have uncovered two very important aspects of this addictive game. First, geneticists have determined that planted in the genes of each individual is the predisposition for certain addiction-producing actions. England, for example, is considering the analysis of young children's DNA to determine if they have a propensity toward addictive drugs such as heroin or cocaine. Secular scientists use these genetic predisposition discoveries to legitimize and rationalize certain behaviors. As secular science uncovers these objective discoveries, its ambassadors erroneously conclude that these actions are simply part of the evolutionary genetic makeup of the human animal. To reinterpret a quote from *The Matrix*: To deny one's genetic impulses *is to deny being human.*

But bringing these discoveries back to our metaphorical game of Russian roulette, we uncover that addiction is not played on a single table. Addiction is birthed out of a number of different repetitious actions. So there are a myriad of tables on which an individual can begin to play, ranging from drugs to pornography, from violence to gambling, and a plethora of other actions. But for each individual, certain guns already are loaded on the table before he begins to play. The guns of drugs and sex may be half full of bullets for one person, while another's loaded gun may be overeating, and another's, child molestation. All the enemy of mankind need do is make sure the right game is well-disguised and enjoyable enough to play so that the individual steps to the table with the right gun (or guns) for his or her genetic predisposition and sits down at the table.

Through clever marketing tactics, progressive ideologies, and mammoth financial capital, not only do these addictive games surround us, but also nearly all tables (all of the addiction-producing actions correlating to mankind's genetic predispositions) are now open and available to play. Even worse, the path to one's addiction table and its preloaded weapons can merely be the click of the mouse or the turning on of a smart phone or tablet.

But through revelations in neuroscience, we learn that the game is further fixed. At the moment of any action, the human brain builds up and develops synapses corresponding to that particular course of action. Whether it is the opening of a door, the smelling of a flower or the feeling of feet hitting the pavement during a run, synaptic pathways are produced. The more intense the action or event, the greater the synaptic buildup (and release of neurochemicals) occurs. Once a pathway tied to a certain course of action has been built, the brain's natural inclination is further travel down that pathway. The more one continues in that action, the greater the infrastructure is strengthened to that neuronal pathway – and the more difficult it is to deviate from that course of action.

For example, at the moment of sexual ejaculation, the brain is flooded with the neurotransmitters dopamine and serotonin. Sex doesn't just feel good to the person; it feels great to the brain and correspondingly to the body. But that dopamine and serotonin travel across the neurological paths built from the actions leading up to that moment, as well as the strongest additional pathways. The brain then knows to feel this good again, the same course of action should be taken. At this moment of neuronal and physical ecstasy (ejaculation), the will already enters the first phases of being subjugated by the flesh. And once addictive actions become no longer enjoyable to the individual (through his will) the body and brain still desire and fight for the same effect. Long before the actual physical addiction, or the moment the gun finally goes off, the brain itself already has made it difficult for the individual to the leave the table.

So both before *and* after addiction occurs, the will of the man is still being perpetually dominated by the flesh of the same man.

Though it is not claimed as such, addiction treatment centers are not curing people of addiction. They are attempting to win the battle over the flesh of the individual that has wholly dominated the will of the individual. The person isn't freed of addiction; his or her flesh is once again controlled and restricted, as it should have been in the first place. But during the process leading to addiction, science unveils that the flesh gains further and further dominance. So what are the secular world's best responses to its own scientific discoveries?

One of science's current solutions is to produce pharmaceutical products, in essence to introduce poisons into the body, that reduce the power of the flesh so persons can enjoy addiction-producing actions longer without the same addictive result. Science is poisoning the body instead of recognizing and dealing with the realities of these addiction-producing actions that they themselves have discovered through their own disciplines! These pharmacological solutions come affixed with a massive list of new objective and detrimental physiological consequences. These consequences are stamped on the front of plastic bottles right after the phrase, "side effects include." In many instances these side effects are more destructive to the physiology of the individual than the result of the initial action.

Worse, there are plans by some genetic experts and medical institutions to extract DNA samples of embryonic human life prior to birth. The thinking is that parents can be warned of potentially addictive future behavior patterns, should they decide to terminate the pregnancy. And I already have spoken of the consideration in England to test for genetic predispositions for heroin and cocaine in the young.

But what does science want to do with children that have the genetic propensity? Inject them with these narcotic drugs as children, so that as adults, they no longer desire the pursuit of what they have already been given. The bottom line is that the three best secular solutions to this objective game of Russian roulette are poison, early forced addiction, and death. For the sake of our society, we must demand better solutions.

WHAT WE MUST DO: THE GENESIS OF A PARADIGM SHIFT

Shift I: Elimination of Compartmentalization

We no longer can afford to compartmentalize society. It not only prevents us from recognizing the crucial realities uncovered in this chapter; it also produces more addicted individuals. News programs often describe someone as a "sex offender" as if this is his or her predetermined identity. But the sex offender was first a man who may have merely done what he had always done – looked at porn at his leisure – only soon, a different result occurred. Let's go back to that television program spotlighting pornography addiction once again. While the host listens compassionately to the sad stories of his or her addicted guests, there would no doubt be certain audience members that would compartmentalize by saying, "Well it might have become a dangerous addiction for you, but I'm just fine and healthy with my porn." But based on distorted reality of the definition of insanity (perpetual action, but at the moment of addiction a different result occurs) and the objective discoveries of neuroscience and genetics, this line of thinking is not only asinine; it's also downright dangerous.

The very person who in that moment is bellowing out the healthy aspects of pornography could be an addict, even a sex offender, a month later. The person who simply enjoys partying on Saturday nights may be the next alcoholic the following weekend. The casual Internet gambler may head to Vegas a year later and squander his family's entire life savings. Simply because what he had done over and over again through his will had finally produced a different result through his flesh.

The church is panned by the secular community for being arcane and dogmatic; and is mocked with seemingly distasteful titles such as "fundamental." From a secular point of view, the term "fundamental" refers to individuals whose morality cannot evolve with the changing needs of the society in which they exist. Often those with the loudest anti-fundamental bullhorns flaunt themselves under the supposedly positive banner of "progressive." But we now have been given a glimpse of why mankind's Creator may appear to be so fundamental with his moral declarations. And how the anti-fundamental leanings of the "progressive" are actually cataclysmic to the flesh and therefore cataclysmic to mankind. While the will may not be a fundamental identity, the human body and brain (the flesh) are. When we are seriously ill, we may claim (will) "I am not sick," but the pale color and warm touch of skin, the profuse sweating in the face and the overall compression in posture (flesh) tell otherwise. If we finally admit verbally to what others are seeing visually, we are not being fundamental. We are being truthful.

And that truth can then set us free.

God speaks fundamentally about certain actions (especially addiction-producing actions) not to dominate and restrict mankind, **but to prevent our own physical and genetic (flesh) proclivities from dominating us!** We can further uncover this reality through the use of a biblical metaphor:

All men are like grass, and all their glory is like the flowers of the field. The grass withers and the flowers fall… Surely the people are grass.
(Portions of Is. 40:6-8, NIV)

Man's flesh is described as grass, and the glory of man as the flower of that grass. The enemy knows that if he can destroy the grass, he has by default also destroyed the flower. *Man's pride and accomplishment may be powerful; but man's physiology is weak.*

So God's fundamental laws against certain addiction-producing actions (sexuality, drunkenness, gambling, drug use) speak to the protection of the weak grass – in order to birth the full flower! Over three millennia prior to this moment in history, the prophet Isaiah metaphorically uncovered the process of addiction, the enemy's tactics, and God's reasoning behind His commands. And it is through the objective findings of secular science that the validity and power of this verse materialize. In other words, through the lens of scientific discovery, this verse opens up a myriad of new objective societal solutions.

Shift II: Recognition of the flesh over the will

In five words, the Creator of mankind unlocked why He must be fundamental when it comes to His creation: "...surely the people are grass." Going back to the verse prior, God is declaring for all of science to hear, process and respond: Surely the people are more physiology (objective flesh) then loveliness (subjective will and accomplishment). We must create a paradigm shift in society. We must recognize that man is not a subjective entity of will, but an objective entity of flesh.

And we must show in repeated, exacting and concerned detail how every subjective decision of the will produces objective consequence in the flesh.

Thankfully, through this scriptural metaphor we not only have the keys to unlock our human realities, but also the reality of God our Creator. God's law systems speak to the subjugation of the flesh (grass) for the fulfillment of the loveliness of the flower (the accomplishment of man through his unconquered will). Conversely, the casualties of addiction are withered grass never able to bud into its intended potential as flowers. And the nihilism in our society, especially in the young, is the result of a generation never having seen the beauty of the flower, since our nation – through the sanctioning of addiction-producing actions – is little more than a collective of withered grass. And what does nihilism foster? Apathy. A disturbed sense of numbness desperately looking for something, anything, to fill the emotional and physical void. And what fills that void most quickly?

Addiction-producing actions.

Once again, we uncloak a perpetual system of destruction being covertly utilized by the enemy of mankind, grounded in scientific reality, warned of in scripture, and staved off by adherence to God's law. By its very nature, proven through our own sciences, the only safe solution is to avoid the table all together. That, dear reader, is not fundamental; that's truth.

The three best secular solutions attempt to sanction the subjective will, and in doing so, wreak cataclysmic damage on the objective flesh (death is pretty cataclysmic). These secular solutions not only perpetuate the cycle, but also increase the scope and chances of addiction by encouraging the society to sanction more and more "Russian roulette" tables through legislation (legalization of child pornography, drug usage, prostitution, in-state gambling, etc.), leaving the enemy free and clear to craft new perpetually destructive strategies.

Just as the secular society cannot compartmentalize the addicted and the healthy, neither can the Christian compartmentalize the individual from his or her flesh. Again, the will is not weak; mankind's physiology is. See Jesus' own words through this lens: "[T]he spirit indeed is willing, but the flesh is weak." (Matt. 26:41, KJV) By understanding and proclaiming that man is far more flesh than will, new societal standards can be enacted to not only liberate mankind from its own manipulated destruction, but also to unveil the reality of a loving God who is desperately attempting to protect His children.

Shift III: Wake Up!

As Christians we must be the first to wake up. We have been given the tools (the sciences) to diagnose the situation, and the salve (the Biblical Worldview) to remedy the world's addictive ailments. *But instead we attack the ill (the addicted) and leave the salve (the Biblical Worldview solutions) on the shelf until Sunday morning.* On most Sunday mornings it's never used a salve because it's seldom removed from its theological medicine chest. It is not that the world is going to a moral hell in a hand basket, *but that because the church has attacked the ill and not the enemy,* the mechanisms by which to ensnare the flesh have been permanently established all around us (Internet pornography, casinos, medical marijuana outlets, legalized prostitution, etc.). Many of those reading these words have been caught in the battle for the flesh. You have bought in to the unchallenged lie that your repeated actions always will produce a similar result. But as Christians we must first petition God to liberate us from our own flesh so that we can become ambassadors of these critical realities.

> ... *[B]ut I discipline my body and make it my slave, so that, after I have preached to others, I myself will not be disqualified.* (1 Cor. 9:27, NASB)

Can we change? In a society in which the same organization warning of the deadly dangers of smoking is also selling the product, pessimism can easily beset us. But it begins with destroying the compartmentalized mindset. And it progresses when we stop focusing on merely *that* God said something and begin to uncover *why* He said it. Everyday science is doing the job for us. It is our job to take the findings of science and apply them through the Biblical Worldview. Our failure to do so has not only furthered science's dominion over the societal landscape, but it also has allowed these addictive edifices to flourish unhindered. Science will continue to prove that many of the most addiction-producing actions are, in their initial stages, physiologically and neurologically "beneficial." We can either cower and run from these findings or use them as our greatest ammunition. I hope you will choose the latter.

Chapter 12

THE SUCCESS OR FAILURE OF AMERICA, INC.

Ponder:
Of what use is money in the hand of a fool,
since he has no desire to get wisdom?
(Prov. 17:16, NIV)

For a moment I'd like you to imagine America universal as its own corporation. We'll call our 300-million-person operation "America, Inc." For this scenario, we will say that America, Inc.'s sole commercial product is this nation's profitable future. Now, strictly from a strategic business perspective, how would we go about making America, Inc. a success? If we followed the standard corporate formula, we would look to others who have made their respective corporations successful. Luckily, when it comes to effective business tactics, there are innumerable resources to help our corporation become highly profitable and lucrative. Millions of individually inspired techniques produce different levels of success. But thankfully there are a few universal truths. Nearly every book on strategic business profitability agrees on a single principle:

For a business to be powerful and effective it must be proactive, not reactive.

A reactive corporation utilizes all its power and time to rectify issues, fix problems and alleviate stresses. It has little or no opportunity to improve its current situation. Why? Because the one commodity a corporation cannot increase is time; it is a fixed asset or it is a serious liability. There are ways to improve time efficiency, but it is impossible to physically extend it. So if a company utilizes all of its resources reactively, it cannot propel forward. All of its potential time to grow is being sucked up by reactive issues. The best it can do is to return to the condition it was in before the breakdown.

More importantly, consider the following two prefixes:

Pro: to continue forward; i.e. "propel," "propigate," "procede"

Re: to move backward: i.e. "retreat," "recede," "remove"

So a proactive corporation always is propelling forward, whereas a reactive corporation is not only underachieving, it also is eroding. What causes a company to be either "proactive" or "reactive?" The methodology relegated down from its leadership. How do we define methodology? Let's go to the dictionary:

Etymology: New Latin methodologia, from Latin methodus + -logia —logy 1: *a body of methods, rules, and postulates employed by a discipline: a particular procedure or set of procedures* (Miriam Webster Online Dictionary, 10th Edition).

The rules, postulates and procedures delineated down from the corporation's leadership become the basis to which all employees of the company must adhere. The more effective at analyzing and isolating potential breakdowns the leadership has been, the more "proactive" the corporation can become. The less effective at analyzing and isolating potential breakdowns the leadership has been, the more they will devote their time, attention and resources to rectifying breakdowns *after they occur*.

Proactive corporations see problems before they occur. Reactive corporations suffer under breakdowns and must then devote attention away from success - and toward *alleviation*.

How does this translate to our corporation, America, Inc.? By not following God's intended desire for humanity's protection through His loving mandates, America, Inc. has become a reactive corporation. Where God saw mankind's destructive outcomes and provided a way to prevent reactive damage, America, Inc. has chosen to reject God's methodology and therefore must react whenever it faces a physical, psychological or social breakdown. America, Inc., being "lawless," or without an understanding of the right methodology and simply viewing and disregarding God's law from a moral context, is reactively wasting its resources of time, money and talent, because physical, psychological and social bondage is inevitable and unavoidable. So if lawlessness becomes the destroyer of potential segments of society, the parts that "lawlessness" does not fully destroy become reactive, hindering proactive successes.

[A]nd sin, when it is full-grown, gives birth to death. (James 1:15, NIV)

The more "lawless" the *actions* of a society become, the more exposed to the *outcomes* of biological, psychological, social and spiritual damage it suffers, and therefore the more reactive the individuals in that society must be. So a society that gives in to what the Bible refers to as "sins," increases the wealth of those that either reactively alleviate the bondage or attempt to anesthetize its reality. Let me say it even more simply:

The more a culture sanctions the actions of sin, *the more it makes rich those that deal with sin's outcomes: the lawyers, doctors, psychologists, pharmaceutical companies, entertainment moguls, alcoholic beverage corporations, casinos, etc.*

Let's quickly look at one "sinful" area in question: pornography. On the secular societal surface, pornography appears to be somewhat benign. Although it is a very lucrative business, the average user, with even the remotest amount of ingenuity, can usually view anything he or she desires at relatively no cost. But cost comes into account quickly when porn does what porn is intended to do: ensnare and divide. Consider the following, from a May 2011 blog on HuffingtonPost.com:

> "At a 2003 meeting of the American Academy of Matrimonial Lawyers, two-thirds of the 350 divorce lawyers noted that the Internet was playing an increasing role in marital splits, with excessive online porn watching contributing to more than half of the divorces. According to Richard Barry, president of the association, 'Pornography had an almost nonexistent role in divorce just seven or eight years ago.'"[1]

So who becomes rich after porn accomplishes its real purpose? First the lawyers: the average divorce costs around $15,000 but costs go up quickly when the separation gets messy. If the family is successful or one of the spouses is an entrepreneur, more time, and therefore, more money must be expended. Then there is the potential psychological damage on the spouses and/or children. The Huffington Post, in an unrelated article, also stated that: *Children of divorced parents are **seven*** *times more likely to suffer from depression.*[2] We can assume that a good counselor is going to be about $75-$125 per hour and a therapist can be even higher. That doesn't take into account the money shelled out on the pharmaceuticals necessary for physiologically coping with the breakup. Then there are the potential medical conditions that arise after divorce: overeating, drug usage and abuse, suicidal proclivities, anxiety, etc. Should any of those cause additional physiological complications (addiction, heart disease, organ failure, etc.) that will require huge amounts of additional money.

This then affects the success of the surrounding community, because usually after a divorce the lifestyle of the former couple drops dramatically. That can mean the loss of a sale of a new car at the Lexus dealership that one party can no longer afford on a single salary. Or it can be as practical as hindering the success of Starbucks when one or both parties can no longer budget in a daily $7 latte habit. This says nothing about the educative and future success of the children. Although no fault of their own, when the children's grades suffer, future opportunities both in the education and the corporate marketplace can suffer as well. This could go on and on, and that's just for something as supposedly benign as pornography, from divorce statistics a decade old.

By its very logic, the more reactive the society, the more it must adopt reactive measures and dole its money out to those who can address the damage. But this in itself is a short-sighted strategy, because as the society perpetuates "reactively," it is imploding from the inside. For those running these reactively alleviating companies have children, friends, parents, etc., that are most likely suffering from the very things they are attempting to alleviate. Just because you are a doctor, lawyer or psychologist doesn't mean your family and friends are exempt from the reactive strategies of sin's outcomes.

The corporation or society eventually self-eradicates once all its resources have been used to "react" to breakdowns. Since it can't acquire more time, it must produce more money. And once it runs out of money, what can it do *but borrow?*

But a proactive society, when it understands and adopts a methodology that circumvents breakdowns, immediately becomes immeasurably more powerful and profitable than a reactive society! Because it now can capitalize on the resources that had been stolen from "reactive" damage control.

Prosperity shifts from the reactive to the proactive; it is once again, as God intended it, bestowed to those that are focused on GROWING the society, because they no longer are shelling out most of their hard-earned dollars to reactive agencies. The growth and prosperity of the society is exponential, because man is free to grow technologies and ideas that address sin's aftereffects of bondage proactively. And should that society embrace "wisdom" as the verse at the beginning of the chapter states, its people, now equipped with a greater understanding of sin's "strategies," can live in even greater prosperity. Disengaging from sin doesn't take money; it takes a changed heart and an illuminated mind. But as believers addressing a skeptical and disinterested world, we make the most impact by exposing the outcomes of sin, not by simply decrying its sinful actions.

So if there is an enemy of mankind, as the Bible asserts, his goal also would be to create a reactive society, which over time would implode (consider Greece, Rome, etc). Sin, once again, becomes the catalyst to building a reactive society; God's system of liberation is the catalyst to building a proactive society. On the very basis of exponential fiscal increase and freedom, God's loving mandates become the financial savior of a society. Now that's relevant!

Unwitting man looks for immediate self-serving of his own agenda (which is what got us here in the first place) based on his desire for his three main entrapments: *the lust of the flesh, the lust of the eyes, and the pride of life.*" (1 John 2:16, NIV) But the enemy always is focused on the end-game result: a state of destruction, stagnation and reactivity. At first this happens at the individual level, but it moves to the corporate level quickly – and purposefully.

But a society that adopts God's loving mandates will by its very nature become the most powerful nation on the planet, because its private and financial resources would be diverted from reactive fiscally draining solutions to proactive society-strengthening agendas. And then, in its abundance, it can see clearly to address the rest of the world's concerns. What the government cannot do through its programs, agendas and solutions, God did – once again – through His desire for humanity's holistic prosperity.

1. http://www.huffingtonpost.com/vicki-larson/porn-and-divorce_b_861987.html

2. http://www.huffingtonpost.com/2010/11/03/higher-depression-rates-children-divorce_n_778506.html

Chapter 13

THE SAFETY OF THE THICKET

Ponder:
A lion has gone up from his lair,
a destroyer of nations has set out.
(Jer. 4:7, NIV)

Growing up in the concrete jungles of California, I wasn't privy to too many thickets – or lions either, for that matter. I have, however, seen the thickets of Africa on numerous animal shows and in vivid color on the pages of picturesque nature books. An African thicket is a tall, dense group of thorn-covered bushes, dried brush and thistles so entangled that it is nearly impossible to see what might be hidden inside. For a young or fragile animal, the thicket is, for the most part, impenetrable. Razor-sharp thorns and drought-hardened sticks are ready to lacerate the skin with little effort. For the weaker animals of the African plains, thickets are places to be avoided, provided one isn't intentionally looking for injury or entrapment. However, if you're an animal with immense strength and extreme determination, thickets are a great place for hiding. And a lion obviously fits this bill. From the stealthy locale of a thicket, a cunning lion easily can lock onto a potential target relatively unnoticed. Before the prey has registered the full scope of danger, the lion has leapt from its concealed position, overtaken the animal and made its kill.

But exposure presents a new problem for the lion. Once the lion is out in the open, the rest of the animals inevitably will scatter. During the chase and kill, the lion is visible to all the other potential game upon which it might hope to gorge at a later time. Strategically, it is best for the lion to attack swiftly and then drag the carcass back to a safe, inconspicuous hiding place. This ensures that the lion has plenty of time to eat the animal in seclusion and, when hunger pangs re-manifest, repeat the process once again. Even with such stealthy tactics, the average lion still only manages a kill ratio of about 20 percent; for every 10 attempts, eight potential dinners manage to escape. Anyone, including the lion, can see those are not very good odds. But a lion has a much higher percentage of successful kills in the dark. Under the shroud of blackness, the lion is much more adept than most of its prey. Springing quickly and catching its prey nearly unaware, the lion is able to snatch a member of the herd, with few even aware of the kill, then fade back into the darkness to revel in the catch. In either case, covertness is the key.

But that is not the picture of the lion found in this verse. This lion has not left his hiding place for a quick covert kill, nor is he stealthily attacking under the cover of clandestine darkness. This particular lion is moving around *exposed in the daylight* and for an *extended period of time.* "Alah" is the Hebrew denotation for the English phrase, "gone up." Its numerous definitions include, "to arise, excel, restore, mount up, perfect, grow, to increase," among its unique descriptors. These definitive expressions indicate that this particular king of the beasts is no longer clandestine, but walking boldly, *if not defiantly.* He is out in the open, in plain sight of all of those he would hope to soon devour.

Now why would a lion do such a thing?

Strategically, if a lion operates and executes best through *covert action,* what is this lion doing "mounting up" and walking around in plain sight? Isn't he concerned that any potential dinner might turn and bound away at the first perception of his presence? Apparently *he is not.* In fact, he can get even more brazen. Remember 1 Peter 5:8? "The devil prowls around like a *roaring lion?"* Once again, this characteristic doesn't make strategic sense for a lion. Although originally not conscious of his presence, as soon as the lion roars, the animals surely would scatter. What chance does a roaring lion in plain sight have at securing and devouring his prey? Though a well-reasoned question, perhaps the better question to ask would be, "Why?" Why has this lion chosen this particular posture? The following represent the only logical (or illogical) reasons a lion would ever attempt such a seemingly foolish tactic.

Reason 1: He believes he is faster and more powerful than his prey.
The first possible reason is that the lion is certain he is faster and more powerful than his prey. If this reason holds merit, then the lion can boldly parade around the animals, for, despite his obvious appearance in the open environment, his prey lacks any ability to escape. Perhaps the rest of the desert animals are simply lazy, content to

graze in the grass, or frequent the watering holes, with heads face-down in the water, oblivious to the lion's immediate locale. These particular animals prefer to gorge themselves on the provision of the land, and fail to condition their muscles with the strength needed for escape. With his prey choosing to live blissfully unguarded, the lion knows that, despite their "best intentions," he has his pick of game at any given time.

You can watch it instead from the comfort of your burning bed, or you can sleep through the static. (Jack Johnson, "Sleep Through the Static, emphasis added")

Reason 2: The lion's prey no longer considers him a life-threatening enemy.

Despite the fact that the lion kills in plain sight, and that their numbers are slowly decreasing, the rest of the living animals fail to make the connection between the deaths of their fellow wildebeasts and antelope and the lion ripping off bits of the flesh of their own kind, right in front of them. This is a petrifying scenario, but one with substantial scriptural support. Consider the following passages in Isaiah:

You have seen many things, but you to not observe them.... (Is. 42:20a, NASB, emphasis added)

Followed two verses down by the outcome of this lack of discernment:

But this is a people plundered and despoiled; All of them are trapped in caves, Or are hidden away in prisons; They have become a prey with none to deliver them.... (Is. 42:22, NASB, emphasis added)

The animals are *easily consumed*, because although they may have seen the lion, *they have grown oblivious to the danger.* Or perhaps the lion's prey is simply counting on the *law of averages.* Although some of the fellow herd may be mauled as they gaze on, the remaining animals figure the chances that the lion will get one of them are slim. As long as they don't make too much commotion, maybe the lion won't pay them any interest.

Both of these scenarios paint a grim picture of the condition of the animal society. Whether or not either of the preceding two reasons is true, it would seem a very arrogant and foolish way for the lion to operate. Acting in this manner, the lion gives away his tactics. The longer the lion is out in the open, the more the animals around him can begin to learn his patterns and modes of operation. As they observe the strategies of the lion, they possess the ability to use that information for their own protection. Eventually, as the animals begin to collectively understand the nature of this lion, they not only learn his approaches but they can set traps for the lion as well. With the right discernment of tactics and strategies, the hunted becomes the hunter.

All in all, it would seem that due to these adverse situations, the best place for the lion to remain would be in safety of the thicket, or under the cloak of darkness. So why risk it? Why would a lion put itself in such a vulnerable position, even if he could overtake his disoriented, amnesic prey? Why not keep things they way they had always been?

Having lunch with a friend of mine, I was discussing the metaphorical significance of the "lion" and the two prior reasons, eager to share with him the magnitude of the concept. Leaning back in his chair, and taking a sip of his sweat tea, he thought for a moment, and then pensively offered, "There is another reason." His tone and intense connection with what I had just spoken assured me that I needed to listen to what he had to say. As he spoke this third reason he had quickly contemplated, I thanked God that this lunch meeting had taken place; and when the check came, I readily paid for his meal.

Reason 3: At this point in time, staying in the thicket is just too dangerous for the lion.

Imagine that. Prior to this moment in time, the lion was able to stay hidden in the thicket, to be content with covert kills. But now something is on the horizon and the lion knows that in order to deal with the upcoming circumstances, he must come out of hiding. Even if it means his tactics are out for plain sight. Even if it means his prey might learn his strategies. It is too dangerous for the lion to remain hidden. The hope of the lion is that his prey stays oblivious, that he can kill enough that the overall group is weakened, and he must do it quickly. It is a gamble, but for some reason the lion knows that soon his time is up, and despite the costs, he'll risk it. Something has to be done now, for the future contains something so powerful that it means his demise.

SECTION 3: INSPIRATION

Chapter 14

WHAT'S IN YOUR SPIRITUAL TACKLE BOX?

Ponder:
Then He said to them, "Follow Me, and I will make you fishers of men."
(Matt. 4:19, NKJV)

Be diligent to present yourself approved to God, a worker who does not need to be ashamed, rightly dividing the word of truth.
(2 Tim. 2:15, NKJV)

A number of years ago, a friend I was discipling posed a question to me after a church service. I love this guy. Most of his questions were about how to *get out of* doing the various spiritual practices that intentionally result in a believer's growth. This was a similar question. "If the Holy Spirit is the One who speaks through me when I witness to someone," he began, "then I don't really have to study scripture or know too much, because He'll bring the words to me, right?" It was a good thought. After all, scripture does say that we are not to worry about what to say when we are in front of others, for He will give us the words with which to speak.

I thought about it for a second. After a quick prayer, I answered, "Jesus says that we are fishers of men, right?" He'd memorized that one. "Yeah, sure," he said. "Based on your question, you are right," I encouraged,

"The Holy Spirit is the real fisherman... *but the lures come from you.*"

"When you are in moments of evangelism," I continued, "the Holy Spirit delves into your spiritual tackle box and chooses one of the lures you have accumulated through all your study, meditation, life experiences, etc., and uses that lure to fish for men."

We *both* got the revelation.

Whenever we are in front of someone else, unbeliever or even a believer, we are to be constantly listening to the nudge of the Holy Spirit to infuse our dialog. In part, the Holy Spirit makes Himself known and accomplishes His agenda through our *dialog* with others. But He only can use in the present what we already have garnered and cultivated in the past. If all you have in your spiritual tackle box is John 3:16, how many people is the Holy Spirit, through your mouth, going to draw in? A limited number, right? But suppose we have accumulated a myriad of lures through countless hours of biblical study, meditation, humility-infused life lessons and failures, secular and religious books, wise relationships, even movies and television (think about the metaphorical power of *The Matrix*). Then, at any moment, in any circumstance, the Holy Spirit can delve into that tackle box, coat your words with spiritual authority and present them to the listener in language that is relevant, topical and winsome.

And often in those moments, those spiritually infused words produce greater insights about God and His ways than you yourself had prior to opening your mouth. I had never thought about the tackle box analogy until that moment standing in front of my friend. But I had been reading Proverbs every day for that year, and Proverbs is loaded with analogies. That metaphor became a clear picture for me from that day forward. And it placed a new significance and responsibility on everything I watched, studied, listened to and engaged in from that moment on.

It pays to be well rounded. It pays to be a good listener. And the dividends are revealed in the lives of those that are transformed because the Holy Spirit now has ample use of your prior spiritual disciplines.

Chapter 15

PRODUCTION VS. CONSUMPTION

Ponder:
The Words of Agur: *There are three things that will not be satisfied, Four that will not say, "Enough": Sheol, and the barren womb, Earth that is never satisfied with water, And fire that never says, "Enough."*
(Prov. 30:15b-16, NASB)

In my personal devotion time, I try to read the proverb of the day, every day. Being the CEO of a small business, I figure I can use all of the help I can get. Proverbs is a businessman's treasure trove. It offers hard, practical business advice in addition to moral, social, biological, generational and of course, spiritual guidance. Proverbs 30 is recognized as being written by Agur, the son of Jakeh the oracle. Apart from this simple generational eulogy, little else is known about the man.

Agur's writing style radically differs from than that of the writer of the other 30 proverbs. His foray into the scriptures begins with the phrase, "Surely I am more stupid than any man." (Prov. 30:2, NASB) If we attempted to personify him today, he probably would best be characterized by the 1970s television detective Columbo. His evangelism style likely would be to agree with everything someone stated to him, but just before closing the door to leave, he'd turn back, scratch his head and say, "You know, you seem to make sense, but have you ever considered… (insert truth here)." Despite his declaration, you will soon see that this man was far from the stupid fool he exposited himself to be.

Agur spends most his chapter musing about common life experiences as they relate to his own existence and what he has seen during his time on earth. The above passage is one of those reflections. Here he describes four things that are never satisfied or that will never say, "Enough:" Sheol (or the grave), the barren womb, earth and fire.

In the reading of this text – at least once a month – I was content to believe that each of these items was universally similar. After all, the writer himself stated so. It looks as if all four are a part of the same "never satisfied" grouping, right? But just as the spoken words of Columbo always contained an abundance of subtext, so, in fact, does this Agur. It was somewhere around the eighteenth monthly reading that this passage exploded open with profound clarity. It is true that all four things here are never satisfied. The difference is in *what they are never satisfied with*. Two are never satisfied with how much they *consume*, and two with how much they *produce*.

The grave and fire are never satisfied with how much they *consume*. They are, by nature, the ultimate consumers, leaving nothing of value in their wake. The grave offers nothing; it swallows life, removing it from existence. It continues perpetually in its consumptive desire. Fire also offers nothing of value in return; it is the ultimate in selfishness, "feeding" only on its desire, and taking air, human life, ecology and beauty with it, until it is brought under control or runs out of consumable material.

The other two, by contrast, are never satisfied with how much they *produce*. The barren womb is never satisfied with being barren, it longs to produce, to bring forth life. Cyclically, the life that it brings forth produces additional life, and so on and so forth. Although it may seem that the earth is "selfish" for desiring such never-ending quantities of water, this is simply the primary source for the production of further abundant life. The earth always wants more water, not for itself, but for the production of trees and plants, the nourishment of animals and humans, the protection of fish, and the list goes on and on. All four could be deemed selfish, but two are selfish about *taking* and two are selfish about *giving*.

Better yet, we could say that two are inwardly selfish and two are outwardly selfish. So it is not the nature of selfishness that is the problem, but what the intent of that selfishness is. If you had a close rich friend who was never satisfied with how much he blessed you with financially, would you consider that person to be selfish? By comparison, if you had a neighbor that you knew stored sugar by the barrel full and never had any for you, despite your repeated petitions for a cup, would you consider him selfish? The difference is that the first person (like the earth or the womb) is outwardly selfish and the neighbor (like the grave and fire) is inwardly selfish.

THE DEEPER QUESTION

We now can take this passage far beyond the biblical text and apply it to every aspect of our lives. Are we, as individuals, focused on consumption or production? Do we live our lives inwardly or outwardly? To answer that question requires some serious and somber self-analysis. Consider writing a list of everything influential in your life, from your relationships, to your home, to your car, to your entertainment choices, to your personal time. Then ask yourself the question: "Are these things in my life primarily about production or consumption?" Are good, new and fresh things coming out of these choices? Or are they predominantly designed for my own self-satisfaction? Then look at your daily interactions: are your conversations with others designed to produce in the lives of those that are listening? Or are you using those conversations to build yourself up or to focus the attention in your direction?

The beautiful thing about this passage is found in the revelation that these aspects of your life may not be glaring sins (or, missing the mark of God's intention), but instead simply are actions, acquisitions and attitudes that consume rather than produce. Remember, the grave and fire are *never satisfied;* so too are the things in our lives that predominantly consume. They will continue to gain more and more dominance, unless we make a conscious decision to turn in a different direction.

For me, this not only required a detailed analysis of my own life, but a daily, if not hourly, conversation with God about the *intent* of my conversations and actions. Every hour, I would go back to God, inquiring, "Was that last hour for Your glory (production) or was it for my own self-benefit (consumption)? Eventually, hours turned into days, and days into weeks, until I developed a *lifestyle* of production. For me, there is no greater feeling than having others affirm your productive lifestyle by sharing that your outwardly focused words have changed their lives.

Thanks to Agur, and his well of wisdom, you have now been given a gauge to measure every aspect of your life, every facet of your conversations. Will you live a life, like the grave and fire, full of selfish and perpetual consumption? Or will you live a life, like the earth and the barren womb, filled with life-giving vitality and production?

Chapter 16

READING THE BIBLE WITH THE DIRECTOR'S COMMENTARY ON

Ponder:
But very truly I tell you, it is for your good that I am going away. Unless I go away, the Advocate will not come to you; but if I go, I will send him to you.
(John 16:7, NIV)

All Scripture is God-breathed and is useful for teaching, rebuking, correcting and training in righteousness,
(2 Tim. 3:16, NIV)

For the word of God is living and active and sharper than any two-edged sword, and piercing as far as the division of soul and spirit, of both joints and marrow, and able to judge the thoughts and intentions of the heart.
(Heb. 4:12, NASB)

One of the most utilized DVD special features is the director's commentary option. Watching a film with the feature enabled allows the viewer the rare opportunity to "hear" the creator, director or writer describe the film in new ways and terms. As each scene unfolds, those having written, directed, produced or starred in the film shower us with new information, thoughts about direction, joys in certain filming moments, and the reasoning behind the subtle symbolism or turn of events in the story.

By enabling the director's commentary feature, a movie on DVD takes on a whole new meaning. Without the commentary, we only view and experience the surface of the film. But the commentary unlocks a myriad of new and complex layers beneath the movie. It becomes a far more enriching experience, bringing greater depth to both the commentators and their creations. It increases intimacy between the viewer, the creator and the creator's product. It is a moment of joy for the creators as well, for it is their opportunity to share the wonder and labor behind their creations. We experience communication and connection on a far deeper level: through the film we see the creator's product, but through the commentary we feel the creator's heart.

Let's break this down a little bit: The first time you see a movie, you are watching it linearly, so the story unfolds with unknown vibrancy and excitement, In that first moment for you, the viewer, the movie is "living and active." You don't know what is yet to unfold; it is a mystery. But once that movie is over it becomes a product. You may discover a few things you missed here and there, but overall it is still the same movie you watched the first time.

But once you see the movie with the director's commentary on, in that moment, it becomes living and active once again. You are given new and fresh revelation about what had once seemed like nothing more than a product. Again, there is mystery and excitement. Still, after that first viewing with the commentary, the movie becomes a product once again.

But...

If you were to daily watch that film with the producer, director and storywriter sitting in your living room, bestowing new information on you every time you watched it, that movie would always remain "living and active," because its authors and creators constantly would shower you with more insights beyond the product of the story. Each time you watched it, you would experience more and more mystery, be exposed to greater insights and mine hidden layers of the film.

UNLOCKING THE DEEPER PARALLEL

It is easy for Christians to view the Bible as a product. We consider it a very crucial, even essential, product, but a product nonetheless. We focus on the surface of the text, remaining passive observers of the writing. We read the Bible like we used to watch films: content that what is right in front of us is all there is. But the Bible was never intended as a product. Nor were Christians to remain content with mere passive observation. The third scripture at the beginning of this chapter states that the Word is "living and active." But instead of simply accepting these words, we can use the parallel above to help validate the claim and extract its deeper meaning. For I propose that the Bible also might have a director's commentary feature, and through its engagement God's Word and God's world will explode with new relevance and purpose.

Why?

Because the Holy Spirit, who indwells all believers, also is the inspired author of the Bible.

The second scripture (2 Timothy 3:16) describes the biblical text, and specifically its supernatural production. The verse states that the scriptures were "God breathed." Other translations of the verse unveil that scripture was "inspired by God." In his original 1828 dictionary, Noah Webster defined "inspiration" as:

"The infusion of ideas into the mind by the Holy Spirit; the conveying into the minds of men, ideas, notices or monitions by extraordinary or supernatural influence; or the communication of the divine will to the understanding by suggestions or impressions on the mind, which leave no room to doubt the reality of their supernatural origin."

It was the Holy Spirit that "inspired" God's chosen human authors. It was His whisperings they put to parchment. And after Jesus' ascension (Acts 1:9-11), the One who inspired the book (at that point, scrolls) was available to all of mankind. The Spiritual Writer of the biblical text is the same Spirit now indwelling every new creation (2 Corinthians 5:17). Ponder this for a second: if the same Holy Spirit that indwells us is also the writer of the Bible – then we have the capacity to understand the reasoning and history behind His words, should He wish to reveal it. Depth of revelation is tied to relationship. In other words, as our relationship with the Holy Spirit increases, the director's commentary feature of the Bible can be further engaged.

But the Advoacate, the Holy Spirit, whom the Father will send in my name, will teach you all things and will remind you of everything I have said to you. (John 14:26, NIV)

The more we partner with the Holy Spirit, the inspired author of the Bible, the more God can share with us the reasoning behind His text; the subtleties of His stories; the specifics behind His word choices and the correlation between different segments and sections of the Book. And like the director's commentary relationship between creator and viewer, we develop a far richer understanding and appreciation of both the Creator and His Word. We were not only meant to understand the rich surface of the text; we also are meant to discover all of the hidden intricacies and subtle particulars of scripture that <u>only its Author</u> knows. Every time you open the scriptures pray that God helps you read the Book with the director's commentary on.

A QUICK CAVEAT

It is important that this level of hearing be tempered with holistic Biblical Truth and a strong Christian Community. Any revelation must align itself with *the whole* of scripture. In the Civil war, both the North and the South cited the Bible as the reasoning behind their stances for and against slavery. But by filtering ideas, discoveries and causes through the entire lens of scripture we can analyze our revelations across all of God's word, discarding what doesn't resonate with the whole of scripture, or seeking deeper study, meditation and prayer. And we need to establish ourselves in a strong Christian community so that our revelatory ideas can be analyzed and encouraged by others with wisdom and humility. Like the director of the DVD commentary, revelation is God's desire: but He also is a God of order, coherency and, above all, love.

DEEPER STILL....

This then validates that the Bible can truly be the only living and active book on the planet, based on the tenets of the worldview itself. No other belief system claims that its sacred text's inspired author also indwells its readership. The validity of the statement and the worldview is uncovered through its very declarations. Once again we find coherency between God's declaration and the tenets of our faith.

Chapter 17

BOWING BEFORE OTHER GODS

Ponder:
Do not bow down before their gods or worship them or follow their practices.
(Ex. 23:24a, NIV)

Here's a typical translation of the scripture above: "God doesn't want you to worship anything besides Himself for He is a jealous God who hates all the other false gods that are out there, so don't serve anything but Him." It may evoke reverence to some, but it leaves others confused and dejected. It appears to put people in their microscopic place: God is big, and you are not, so serve Him. Consider the following quote again from renowned atheist Richard Dawkins:

The God of the Old Testament is arguably the most unpleasant character in all fiction: jealous and proud of it; a petty, unjust, unforgiving control-freak... megalomaniacal, sadomasochistic, capriciously malevolent bully." (condensed for emphasis)

But look at what really is being said in the scripture above: "Do not bow down." In the days this text was written, you bowed before kings, before people of authority. Or more succinctly, you bowed before people of *more importance* than you. And this type of bow was the ultimate form of submission: to lay prostrate before another person or deity. To say, "I am not worthy to even be in your presence, so I shall bow before you." I suck, but you are worthy.

So what is God really saying in this scripture? Is he forcing some control-freak nature on humanity as Dawkins posited? Or, if we understand "bowing," is he saying something like this?

"Do not consider a single thing in this universe of more importance and of more value THAN YOU... other than Me."

109

What does that do to your personal worth? To your significance as a human being? You are of such ultimate value and richness that you are not to consider yourself less than any other thing in the universe – *but* God. The One who created the cosmos, the beauty of Yosemite, the force behind the waves on the North Shore of Oahu. And all of that creation pales in comparison to your inherent value. Now that's liberating. You matter! You're of immense worth! So much so that the only thing of more worth is God himself. We spend years attempting to motivate ourselves to some semblance of significance and here God is saying you can't even begin to conceive how valuable you are. You, Christian or not, diehard atheist or agnostic, it doesn't matter.

Now, consider the following quote in this light:

> *It is not as in the Bible, that God created man in his own image. But, on the contrary, man created God in his own image.* (Ludwig Feuerbach)

How pathetic. Not in terms of this man or his quote, but in terms of your significance and worth. If there is no God, if you are just "lucky mud," an accidental blip in this cosmic comedy, then you have such limited value. If we can't think up anything bigger than ourselves, then how can we see ourselves as more majestic than the really beautiful things that surround us? No wonder the world is racked with nihilism and despair.

If you see God as a demagogic ruler, then the natural inclination is often to fight that authority. But if you can see just how valuable you really are, you can begin to revere your self and your Creator in a new light. God sees us as the most valuable entity in the universe other than Him; it is time to for us to get up from whatever we have bowed down to and start to recognize and act on that powerful revelation. And then we not only worship out of recognition of His value to us, but also out of our immense value to Him.

Chapter 18

THE HARVEST IS ALREADY HERE!

Ponder:
Don't you have a saying, 'It's still four months until the harvest'? I tell you,
open your eyes and look at the fields!
They are ripe for harvest.
(John 4:35, NIV)

Church leaders often speak of the "harvest." Loosely translated, it is seen as a moment in history that ushers the throngs of the unsaved into salvation, and therefore into heaven. Under this mindset, it is a time that has not yet happened. It is something to attain. Churches hold conferences, prayer summits and fasts in an effort to usher in the moment of great harvest.

But Jesus stated plainly that the harvest already was around us. All we needed to do was to open our eyes to see it. I believe that to open our eyes to Jesus' statement is to understand the very nature of the term. So returning the term "harvest" to its simple roots, what do we discover?

The "harvest" is the moment that what originally was seeded is finally utilized for its intended potential.

A farmer sows seed with an end in mind. He does not sow to watch stalks grow. He plants his seed specifically for the moment of future harvest. It is what is on his mind from the minute he plants, and it dominates his thoughts through all the work necessary to see his seed grow full and strong. Harvest is the moment that his intent for the seed is realized, or "harvested," and subsequently utilized.

Stepping back into the scripture, if Jesus' harvest metaphor was talking about people, then when were we, as people, first "seeded?" It was the moment of your birth. Biblically, when God makes reference to man's birthing substance (I'm being discrete) He refers to it as his "seed." The very word in Greek for seed is "sperma." It's where we get the English term "sperm."

Despite what you may have been programmed to believe, your life is no accident. Nor was it just the genetic luck of your two parents. God, in his infinite wisdom and intention, knew you and "seeded" you on this planet:

> *Before I formed you in the womb I knew you.* (Jer. 1:5a, NIV)

But through the harvest metaphor we now see that each of us was seeded for a purpose. Harvest is not just about salvation; it's about divine purpose and intent. Remember, it is the moment that a seed is utilized for its *intended* potential. Therefore, we can create a new definition for *spiritual* harvest.

Spiritual harvest would be the moment that a person (which God first seeded) is recognized for his or her God-given potential, and his or her God-ordained traits, talents and abilities begin to be cultivated and utilized for the glory of God.

Each one of us has been blessed with God-given talents, ideas, personality traits and even idiosyncrasies having been placed there by God to be harvested and used for His glory and His workmanship. There are things that you alone are uniquely equipped to do, and God "implanted" these things inside you to be uncovered and cultivated. Salvation is the gateway, but it is not the moment of harvest. Harvest occurs when you begin moving in your God-specific and intended potential. All your passions, desires and traits collide and in everything you do you start feeling His wind beneath your wings, all for His glory and recognition.

This creates a huge paradigm shift in the role of those in spiritual leadership. It certainly is not to have a large congregation. It is not to fill positions in the children's ministry, or the choir or the hospitality staff. It is about getting down and dirty, just like a farmer, and unearthing the intent of the lives of those God has placed under your care. It is to find each person's "God-purpose," and to encourage and empower them to walk in it. And you can use every arsenal at your disposal to do it, be it prayer, worship, teaching, study and even financial provision.

As a Christian, it is your blessed opportunity to see those around you through the same mindset: to lovingly peer into the lives of others and discover, unlock and propel the very reason God seeded them here as well.

For you personally, it might be a vocational change or the pursuit of dream that just won't seem to go away. It *could* be a call to the ministry or the mission field. But it might be a shift from being an accountant to becoming a schoolteacher, if that is the specific role God has ordained for you to reveal His light to the world. It could be the recognition that everything about you — yes, even your idiosyncrasies — has been designed by God to be utilized for a purpose.

Imagine a city of Christians who have discovered and are operating in their "God-purposes," people who have unlocked *the very reasons* they were born and are selflessly helping others do the same. Imagine a community of people who have been harvested and are helping to increase that harvest. What impact would that have on the rest of the community? On the rest of the world?

The harvest is already here. If you're a pastor or leader, the harvest has first been brought to you through the lives of your membership. If you are a Christian, the harvest is sitting in the office cubicle next to you, living next door, or working out on the StairMaster beside you. Salvation is the entrance. After all, God's initial intent is for the salvation of all. But through this new understanding of the harvest, we discover it's just the beginning.

Chapter 19

THE POWER OF "RENEWAL"

Ponder:
Do not conform to the pattern of this world, but be transformed by the
renewing of your mind. Then you will be able to test and approve what
God's will is – his good, pleasing and perfect will. (Rom. 12:2, NIV,
emphasis added)

In the early 1990s, late-night cable television, still suffering from a lack of original programming, often gave up its early morning timeslots to a marketing phenomenon known as the "infomercial." A product sales-pitch disguised in the form of a thirty-minute entertainment special, infomercials offered product creators the opportunity to display the wonder of their products through real-time, real-world situations. One particular infomercial opened with the host and the product creator taking a visit to local auto junkyard in hope of finding a vehicle coated in weather oxidation and rust. The chosen vehicle was an eyesore, having been left to rot in the junkyard, far from its previous owner's memory – abandoned, discarded and devalued. The harsh treatment of the weather and the elements had left what appeared to be irreparable damage on nearly every portion of the vehicle's surface.

But that was only the beginning of the show. Once the product's creator applied his special wax-like compound to the damaged paint surface, the original brilliance and color of the vehicle started to shine through once again. Soon, what had been destined for scrap and removed from remembrance appeared just as pristine at it had on the showroom floor. The creator simply used his revolutionary product to renew the vehicle back to its original and intended beauty.

It is interesting to note that the scriptural passage above states we are called to "renew" our minds. Often we consider – and even dismiss – this scripture as far too difficult a proposition. But this is because we fail to analyze what really has been said. We are not called to "make our minds new," but to "renew our minds." So what is the difference? To renew something, requires that at some point it was new, or operating in its intended usage. Just like the vehicle in the infomercial, we are not struggling to accomplish something foreign to our nature; we are actually bringing our mind into alignment with its intended operation. In other words, through this "renewal," we are bringing our mind back to its original state. In that state, we think, see and act from a perfect, pre-fall mindset of the world.

But why does this "renewal" appear so foreign to us, more like a distant dream than a tangible reality? Because at birth, we are not "showroom quality;" we are not new. The Bible states that we are born into a world of sin and death. We are exposed to the elements from our first breaths. But that's not the way the Creator intended it. God's creation of man at the beginning was more than "good;" it was "perfect." But man, cajoled by the enemy, thwarted that plan. So God sent His Son, in order that we could be "born again," and reopened to the possibility of our intended purpose. It is through the renewal of our minds that possibility turns into reality. We all enter our new life heavily oxidized, badly worn down by the harsh elements. Much of this oxidization has occurred through what we have let into our eyes and ears. We can't see it, but we know it's there – leaving us with a discolored apathy toward our potential and leaving other stimuli (drugs, alcohol, sex, addiction, entertainment, etc.) to fill the void. Much of the world feels as if it has been left in the junkyard, abandoned, discarded and devalued.

But through the renewal of our mind, we can, for the first time, align ourselves with our intended purpose and bring our mind back to its original state. In the beginning, the renewal effort appears agonizing if not impossible. Like applying compound to oxidation, the oxidized surface grows so accustomed to the damage it doesn't give up easily. But as the encrusted layers begin to break apart, the process steadily becomes easier as more of the renewed surface is exposed. Prayer, meditation and fasting are much like "spiritual" compounds, designed to break away at the layers of false oxidation, and expose you to the true beauty, power and purpose that your life was designed and destined for. Remember that the infomercial creator's product only was purchased and praised <u>after</u> the product had accomplished its result on the oxidized automobile. The powerful evidence of your renewal will be an inspiring example to others. Your renewed illumination will point the oxidized masses to the Creator's product... and the Creator Himself. And our internal spiritual renewal, as you will see in the coming chapter, is a catalyst to *furthering the Creator's storyline.*

Chapter 20

FURTHERING THE CREATOR'S STORYLINE

Ponder:
*In their hearts humans plan their course, but the
Lord establishes their steps.*
(Prov. 16:9, NIV)

"It's all about the story…."

So says industry-renowned scriptwriter and professor Tom McKee in his acclaimed book, *Story*. Writing to aspiring screenwriters and authors of fiction, McKee warns that the most critical component of a fictional script or novel is not its characters, settings, events or dialogue; it is the storyline itself. Without a well-developed and engaging storyline, even the most intriguing characters eventually fall flat. For the writer, the storyline is what propels his or her work forward, and every character, event and circumstance must tie back to the writer's ultimate storyline. Though we marvel at our television and movie actors and talk for days about a film's special effects or humor, in the writer-created fictional world, McKee still asserts: "It's all about the story."

I would like to argue that daily living is also all about the storyline. And in nearly identical manner to the fiction script, every individual, event and circumstance in your life holds immense meaning and purpose. In just a few short minutes I can uncover how your daily existence can open up with such richness and providential purpose that your life will be more dramatic than any character you ever have seen or enjoyed on film or television.

I understand that the last paragraph may sound like rhetoric or hype. In fact, I cannot make these assertions inside the current Christian standard of thought. My claim will not sync with most of Christianity's currently marketed literature or its weekly teachings.

Amidst the sea of books designed to produce your best life now and the countless manuals and sermons unlocking the keys to personal success through biblical principled living, the materializing theme of 21st century Christianity is the effective use of God and His principles to further YOUR personal storyline.

There are countless Christian instructors waiting in the wings to divulge God's biblical secrets for achieving personal goals, once a believer has decided the chosen path for his or her life. Skilled teachers stand ready to show the individual how to mine the Bible for the principles necessary to become the best doctor, lawyer, CEO, husband, friend, father, student, ad infinitum, this side of heaven. In essence, much of 21st century Christianity says that you have a personal storyline, and that God has given you the keys to help fulfill that story, as well as a communication line directly to Him when your story gets rough or confusing. Once a believer has fulfilled his or her personal storyline through the help of Providence and His principles, the ultimate expression of thanks is to give God the final glory.

There is nothing necessarily wrong with this vein of Christian thought. In fact, it must be backed with a hefty amount of biblical support, or it could not have so many advocates. But it *is* spiritually anemic and personally narcissistic. And it offers little of what the rest of world desperately seeks. Furthermore, it is impossible to make the bold assertions above through the lens of 21st century Christianity; your life only can become as grand as you have the capacity to make it, even with Providence's help. This is why we idolize screen actors and music artists from the fictional story world, but do not ultimately admire the lives of daily citizens, apart from a few rare pastors, CEOs, and maybe extreme altruists like Bono or Mother Teresa. The story world is far more exciting and expansive than daily existence. This is, in part, why the average American spends 8.1 hours watching television stories instead of cultivating his or her own.

Thankfully, however, there are two ways for a born-again Christian to live. Surprisingly, they are diametrically opposed to each another:

You either can live to insert God into your personal storyline, or you can live in such a manner that God inserts you into His.

The latter choice doesn't come pre-packaged with nearly as much instructional literature. It is impossible to standardize. There is no exacting formula for inclusion. Although I can't divulge a formula or standard, I can give you a whole genre that proves its reality and necessity. It is the genre of story and script writing. And by simply dissecting a few standards of story writing through the lens of the true

Biblical Worldview, I promise you will never see the Creator, the storyline, or yourself in the same way again. And when we are done, you'll see that the best life you possibly could imagine will pale in comparison to the life that Providence is expectantly waiting to give you. How can I be so sure? Because the radically dynamic, Providentially influenced life you specifically were designed to experience is not just "all about the story;" it's all about furthering the Creator's storyline.

STARTING WITH THE FICTIONAL STORY

Let's begin with a look at one of television's most dynamic series, the counter-terrorist, real-time thriller *24*. *24* details the life of former Counter Terrorist Unit Director Jack Bauer (played by Kiefer Sutherland) and his cohorts at CTU-Los Angeles as they work tirelessly to unlock clues and dissect extreme situations of national security. Every second of each 24-hour season is fully utilized (both by Jack and by the viewing public) as Jack and the team attempt to thwart whatever diabolical terrorist agenda has been launched on an unsuspecting public. Sometimes, Jack's situation appears hopeless, until "happenstance" steps in. Let me give you some examples:

A character necessary to solving the particular conspiracy has been shot and left for dead. But the character manages to cling to life just long enough for Jack to arrive so he can whisper to Jack the six-digit access code to a currently unbreakable computer terminal.

Or, with all leads totally exhausted, Jack and crew leave the staging house of one of the major terrorist conspirators empty-handed and without a single future suspect. But Jack "just so happens" to leave something in the house and decides to return to retrieve it. As he searches for the lost item, a hidden cell phone "happens" to ring, and Jack and the CTU team are able to track the call and begin searching for the next previously undiscovered terrorist in line.

My personal favorite came during the second season. After a nuclear device is discovered in Los Angeles, Jack bravely volunteers to fly the device into the uninhabited desert on a suicide run, since he is the most qualified person to complete the job. As Jack's plane nears the planned detonation zone, one of his superiors who "just happened" to have been irradiated earlier in the day jumps from his hiding place, forcing Jack to parachute off the plane. Jack is once again "miraculously" saved while his already dying superior mans the plane to its target point and saves Los Angeles from nuclear disaster.

Now to us as viewers (and to Jack), these little "coincidences" and "fortunate turns of fate" are supposed to appear random and uncoordinated. All appears lost, but thankfully a turn of events gets Jack back on track. We need to recognize that each of these events of "happenstance" actually is a key component of a standard of effective story development: Every situation, event or character must propel a story toward a final fruition. And, more importantly, every sequential scene and circumstance must directly tie back to the ultimate storyline.

"PROVIDENTIAL" STORYTELLING

From a storytelling standpoint, Jack is not just the lead character of the television program. He is the central character to furthering the creator's storyline. And the story's creator, the developer of a story's world, is more than just its writer. The creator (or writer) acts as providence in that world, since the writer has created the world through which all events and characters play out. In essence, the story-writing creator acts as god in his own created world. This providential discovery reveals the critical importance of the relationship between creator and character. Because Jack is the central character furthering the creator's storyline, the story's creator must continuously act "providentially" in Jack's life. Every situation and event of "happenstance" during Jack's 24-hour day (one full season) must carefully and meticulously be crafted by the story's creator. Why? Because each providential event helps accomplish the creator's agenda: the finished telling of his or her story. Remember, as McKee said, it's all about the story.

We can then see how a story's providential creator determines the hierarchy and accomplishments of his or her story's other supporting characters: The more central the character is to the creator's storyline, the more providential the creator must be in that character's life. Secondary and tertiary characters do not receive the same amount of providential assistance. Why? Their personal agendas are not as harmonious to the overall storyline. We don't follow Chloe, one of the CTU computer whizzes, everywhere she goes in the story world of 24. We merely engage her now and then as her character once again becomes central, not simply to Jack, but to the creator's storyline. But Jack's life continuously is providentially assisted, because Jack's sole focus and agenda is the furthering of the creator's plan and intent for the overall story. Stepping outside that plan and intent does not eliminate a character from the overall storyline; it merely reduces the need for the story's providential creator to deliberately act on that character's behalf.

STEPPING INTO A BIGGER STORY

We now can apply this "creator/storyline/character" understanding to the Ultimate Creator of the Biblical Worldview. Several months ago I had coffee with a young college student I had befriended years back while he was in junior high and I was a young and inexperienced youth group leader. He had since fed himself on a steady diet of humanistic and nihilistic philosophical literature, existentialist poetry and naturalistic science – the common staples of modern-day academia. The institutes of higher learning had reshaped and remolded what once had been shaped and molded by the church. During the course of the evening he disclosed his current theological stance. "I see God," he began, "as disinterested in the daily affairs of man, having created a mechanistic world he has since grown tired of." His conclusions were based on the "reshaped" life he had chosen for himself and, correspondingly, a visible lack of God in his daily life. Instead of refuting his claim, I replied, "I can completely see why you believe that. Based on your current lifestyle choices, I don't believe it's possible for you to see God any other way."

Too often we contest declarations such as his without understanding those willing to state them are being far more honest than we realize. Like his college professors no doubt had asserted, he was free to choose his own way, to write his own story. But there was little opportunity for Providence *to appear* as if He was acting in my friend's life for his good. His life had become about furthering his own storyline, not the storyline of Providence. His perception of a deistic God was true – based on his personal storyline. He had chosen to become an extra on the set of life. That's the great thing about being an extra on a television show or movie set: Most of your time is your own. You pretty much can come and go as you please. But you miss out on the opportunity to be an integral part of an awesome and inspiring story, carrying with it so many benefits an extra fails to experience.

DON'T BLAME PROVIDENCE

Now don't get me wrong. It is not that Providence refuses to operate in the lives of those who choose their own limited storyline. But the actions Providence takes are so antithetical to our personal storylines that His redirection will appear random, chaotic and even detrimental. Let's take that last idea back to *24*. There are plenty of characters written into the *24* script having absolutely nothing to do with the story – until Jack somehow comes crashing into their lives. As they now integrate into providence's (the story writer) overall story,

Jack's events and circumstances often appear highly disadvantageous to the new character's personal agenda. New characters often repeat lines similar to: "I didn't sign up for this," or, "This is not my fight; leave me out of this." Though Providence is constantly attempting to steer and direct each person's life back to its ultimate fullness, His redirect may not appear Providential. Why?

The person in question has chosen to act as providence in his or her own life.

EMBRACING GOD'S STORYLINE MEANS A FULLER/RICHER LIFE

But those choosing to wholeheartedly embrace the Creator's storyline, jumping into Providence's plan with reckless abandon and complete faith, experience lives rich and overflowing with Providential assistance. God, who is infinite, knowing the end from the beginning, the One able to simultaneously view every person, situation and event from creation to eternity, personally will order your steps so as to complete His divine story. This is exactly what a story creator does. A story creator uses his or her characters to further an already completed storyline, even though the characters and the audience participate in the story through linear progression. Every event, subtlety and coincidence has been honed, refined and tested before the action ever takes place on screen.

For we are God's handiwork, created in Christ Jesus to do good works, which God prepared in advance for us to. (Eph. 2:10, NIV)

In *24*, the events and accomplishments for Jack's character were scripted well in advance of his linear progression because Jack is central to the creator's story. In identical fashion, the Bible claims in Isaiah 46:10 that God knows the "end from the beginning," or, based on this metaphor, the necessary quality of a "providential" story creator.

It gets even better. Because the creator develops the "world" of his story and acts providentially through it, everything in that creator's world is at the creator's discretionary means. Not only are Jack's "steps" providentially determined, all of the resources in Jack's world are available to Jack — *as soon* as they correspond to the creator's storyline.

If Jack needs a signed agreement by the President, a nondescript briefcase with $2 million in unmarked $100 bills, or a full weapons package and a team "locked and loaded" in the motorpool in 10 minutes, he gets them. Not simply because Jack asked for these items during the linear story, but because the progression of the creator's storyline requires the use of the resources from the creator's world. In the same way, the true Creator utilizes all the resources of His world in and through the lives of those willing to fully embrace His storyline.

We can again look at Jack to determine why we don't always get what we want – or even need – according to *our own* desired timeframe. Jack only receives each item and resource in the creator's world at the appropriate time necessary for the progression of the creator's storyline. Jack may need $2 million during Hour Ten, but he does not receive it in Hour Two, Five or Seven. It is provided to Jack at exactly the perfect moment of need in the creator's storyline. Again, we discover scriptural support: "Every good and <u>perfect</u> gift is from above." So we now see that both the works and gifts from the Creator's world are given to those whose primary goal is to further the Creator's storyline, and bestowed at the perfect moment of need toward that end.

WHICH ROLE WILL YOU CHOOSE?

The question you must answer is which character you will choose to be. Will you be a secondary character, a tertiary character, or perhaps an extra? Will you ensure portions of your own life are under your total control in your own finite frailty? Or will you strive to be a central character, furthering the development of the Creator's storyline? Choosing to live in such a manner means that the Creator Himself must purposefully orchestrate your steps and provide you all of His natural and heavenly resources because of the critical role you play in His story. Make no mistake; it is a choice. This is the absolute brilliance and the ultimate tragedy of free will. You are blessed and cursed with the ability to do anything and everything you want – and miss the amazing opportunity your life was destined for because Providence was not only cheering you on, He was carefully orchestrating all your steps and providing you every resource.

Remember, this is the God who in a breath spoke the galaxies into existence, designed the vast oceans and mountains we plan months in advance to visit on vacation, carefully crafted the beautiful intricacies of each animal down to the hair follicle, scale or feather and way beyond. What can *you* do?

Let's go back to the story-writing genre once again. When a show garners critical acclaim, who receives the credit for the work? The story writer and director. In the same manner, when the God of the Universe steps into your personal life to further His storyline, the actions and outcome of your life look like the God of the Universe, not mere mortal man. And people will be drawn to you in the same manner as those fixated on the 24-hour season of Jack Bauer because your very life is orchestrated so dramatically and wonderfully different than those around them.

And as the Creator sees us being faithful to further His storyline in our limited spheres of influence, He increases our spheres of influence and resource through His own Providential action.

His master replied, 'Well done, good and faithful servant! You have been faithful with a few things; I will put you in charge of many things....' (Matt. 25:23, NIV)

According to the parable, what were the servants in charge of? The man's personal affairs. Allow another verse to sink in deeply:

And we know that in all things God works for the good of those who love him, who have been called according to his purpose. (Rom. 8:28, NIV, emphasis added)

Without considering this creator/storyline/character relationship, this scripture often leaves secondary, tertiary and extra characters in the story of life confused and decimated. The events in the lives of most Christians do not appear to be working out for the good. But it is because they fail to read the last part of the verse. Just like the story writer pre-determines, for those fully aligned with God's purpose, God must providentially work all things and circumstances in their lives. And instead of having a human, finite writer scripting your life, the all-powerful, infinite God has taken that role.

SO WHAT IS GOD'S STORYLINE?

The answer is radically simple and unbelievably complex. The Bible states there was One who came to this earth not just as the main character of the storyline, but also as its Creator. His name was Jesus, and He was both God's Son (main character) and God (the Creator of the story of existence). Scripturally, He is "the author and finisher of our faith." We attempt to analyze and ascertain Him as a main character, but somehow His storyline as Creator has been often misplaced. Thankfully, Jesus repeatedly affirmed His storyline. He said the Kingdom of Heaven was near.

Jesus understood God's storyline: It was to bring man back to his loving God and give him the glorious opportunity to spend eternity with Him. That is the glory of our future. But there also is glory in the present. For God's desire is to bring His creation (earth) and God's image (mankind) back to His intended purpose *now*: the unbroken story, the reconciliation of both God's creation and image back to its pre-fall – and perfect – state, both physically and spiritually.

> *Rescue those being led away to death; hold back those staggering toward slaughter.* (Prov. 24:11, NIV)

Man proved time and time again that he could not complete this part of the storyline. So the Creator entered back into the storyline, fulfilling its purpose, becoming mankind's new, and perfect, Adam – the new man, the undefiled central character. When Jesus said, "It is finished" on the cross, He essentially was declaring for all of creation, "I have reset my storyline back in order." The Creator, the central character, and the finished storyline had fused.

Now that God has completed His portion of the storyline through Christ, it is time for His image (mankind) to do the same. Through Christ's resurrection and ascension back into heaven, the Creator, now acting as the central character in the fulfillment of the story, calls others to complete the task "on earth as it is in heaven." It is as if Jack Bauer were to come to you and say, "Here's my weapon and my access card to CTU; now it's your turn to act as a central character and further the creator's storyline." If the same Creator is writing the story, then He surely can work the same Providential circumstances in your life, provided you take a central character role. As Jesus said, you will "do even greater things than these." And that is exactly what the Creator is looking for. The Bible says that, "the eyes of the Lord" run to and fro about the earth, to find one whose heart is truly His." What is He searching for? Those who long to be central characters in HIS story.

HOW DO I BECOME A CENTRAL CHARACTER?

To become a central character you intimately must involve yourself with every facet of the Creator's world. Jack Bauer is an engaging story character because of his broad scope of proficiency, including languages, culture, history, tactics, strategy and physical fighting ability. The list goes on and on. In the story world, it's called being a multi-dimensional character. But the sole purpose of a character's multi-dimensionality is the advancement of the creator's storyline! Everything Jack accomplished or learned through his "backstory" life helps further the completion of the creator's storyline. We then can see three of the essential components of becoming a more central character:

You must be a student of God (the Creator), a student of His Word (His storyline), and a student of His world (His story world).

Dive into God, His Word and His world with reckless abandon. Devote yourself to gaining a deeper understanding of who He is through an inspiring time of daily scriptural study, meditation and prayer. Find an enlivening church that is embracing God's storyline. And then become a radical student of the world around you. Engage in politics, study philosophy, jump wholeheartedly into the arts and the humanities – all the while asking God to show you how to use His story world to further His storyline. The more multi-dimensional you become, the more you can engage the world around you with the truth of God, because God is both the Savior and Creator of mankind and the world.

Regardless of where you currently stand ideologically, God has placed you on this planet because you are to have a hand in reconciling the earth and its inhabitants back to their Kingdom state. Part of your calling is to "rebuild the ancient ruins," on this earth, not to sit as an extra and count the days till the Creator removes you from the supposed "tragedy" of the current story, or you attempt to accomplish your own storyline. Our current "God said it, I believe it and that settles it" discriminatory mentality has caused us to remain one-dimensional, flat characters that the world often rejects. Furthermore, it allows mankind to justify its own harmful and erroneous storylines.

Above all, you must seek humility and purity. Without humility we'll never even see the story, and without purity we are annexed from becoming more central in God's storyline. The enemy of mankind, the devil, knows this all to well. It is why so many of today's diversions steal away our purity and force us to become insensitive to the things that grieve God, perpetually distancing us from His storyline.

It will teach you to love what you're afraid of
After it takes away all that
You learn to love. (Jack Johnson, "Hope")

The enemy deliberately has created endless false and damaging storylines to help us lose track of the true story. Worse, he has thrust many of us into painful and abusive backstories we never were intended to participate in, especially at young ages when we were helpless to stand up against them.

If we were to be really honest, we spend the majority of our lives engaged in other storylines, numbed to the damage they cause and naïve to the true storyline we've given up without much as a fight. But that can change. Instead of watching God's storyline unfold despite you, you can be a part of making it happen. You can walk in confidence that, at the end of your part in His earthly storyline, you'll hear, "Well done, good and faithful servant." Becoming a central character in the Creator's storyline is a choice given freely by the Creator to be accepted or rejected through freewill. As C.S. Lewis stated in *The Screwtape Letters,* the enemy of mankind "forces" his will on man; God only "woos." But if you are willing to step into the Creator's storyline and become a central character during your lifetime, God makes this promise:

> *But seek first his kingdom and his righteousness, and all these things will be given to you as well.* (Matt. 6:33, NIV)

The choice is now up to you. Take a moment, clear everything else away and ask yourself which role you will choose to play. The audience of heaven and earth awaits your answer.

Sometimes, being part of the storyline requires a faith you may not have realized, as you will discover in the chapter to follow.

Chapter 21

FAITH, FRODO & POPCORN

Ponder:
Now faith is assurance of things hoped for, the conviction of things not seen.
(Heb. 11:1, NASB)

Have you ever been in a dire situation or circumstance in your life in which prayer appeared to be the only solution? I know for myself, there have been many situations that have seemed insurmountable, and I anxiously cried out to God to free me of my distress. Though God always eventually answers, there are times where I've read the passage above and thought, "Maybe I just didn't have *enough* faith to change my circumstances." After all, Jesus said if we had faith like a grain of a mustard seed we could move mountains, so I must not have gotten to that mustard seed level, right? But maybe it's not that we don't have enough faith, but that we may need to see faith in a different light.

Maybe faith is linear humanity syncing up with a God who knows the end from the beginning.

Let's suppose you just got the DVD set of *The Lord of the Rings* film trilogy. Man, what a series of movies: the action, the effects, what a feast for the senses. You probably watched it two or three times in the theater, and it was well worth the $50 in popcorn and soda you shelled out to do so. But then you discovered you have a friend who (aghast!) hasn't seen the films. So you invite your friend over for a movie marathon. Popcorn and sodas (for a lot less money) on the coffee table before you, you begin the first chapter.

As he or she is watching the film, you revel in their excitement. You've already been there; now it's a joy to see someone else go through it with you. Soon, they've journeyed with Frodo, fought with Aragorn and laughed with Pippin and Merry. And then it happens: the moment where Frodo is struck by the giant spider, Shelob. And for all the

129

wonder of this visual journey you have invested tens of hours into, Frodo falls to the ground dead. What?! The somber music plays, the slow motion camera pans. It's over....

... and your friend is *freaking out.*

The reason for his panicked state of mind is that he or she is watching the film linearly. They don't know what will happen next; to them it is all unfolding before their eyes. But what about you? Are you, once again, clawing at the La-Z-Boy's armrest, anxiously wondering why you threw away another nearly half a day of your life to see your little hero die steps before victory? No, you sit calmly eating your popcorn, smiling at your friend. Why? *Because you know the end from the beginning.* He or she is in a state of panic because they watched the film linearly, and you are calm and collected because you already know what's going to happen three minutes later. (Spoiler alert, Frodo lives.) You, watching that movie, transcend time.

This is how we need to see our relationship with God when it comes to circumstantial prayer, and it also better explains how faith works. Whenever we are in a circumstance that seems difficult or impossible, we often pray for God to get us out of the situation. In doing so, we invite him into our linear timetable; to see the circumstance the way we see it. But God isn't linear. He transcends time. He already knows when the circumstance will turn itself around. He's seen it ahead of time. As we cry out, "God will this ever end!" He's sitting there smiling, with His box of popcorn saying, "What are you talking about? It'll all be over in two weeks!" He's already looking at our victory, even as we are crying out to see our linear tragedy transformed.

And here's where faith comes in. Faith is seeing the circumstance from God's perspective; believing that we too can see the end from the beginning. Instead of praying for God to get us out of circumstances, pray that God can help us see the situation already remedied, just as God sees it. Faith is asking God to help us sync to His time-transcendent nature and not to see the circumstance through our own linear lens.

This also shifts the attitude with which we pray. Instead of crying out with frustration and anxiousness, we celebrate the victory that already happened, *with* God. We rejoice in what He already has done, what He already has seen. Remember: faith is the proof of things "unseen" – linearly. We believe and act like He's *already* seen it.

This also speaks to relationship. When your friend sees Shelob skewer Frodo, in that panicked state, where does he or she look for answers? To you. Your friend is either comforted or further distressed based on your facial and body expression. The more trust they have in you, the more assurance they have that your response to the situation is the right one.

Faith is... the <u>assurance</u> of things hoped for.

We are assured because we have built up a deeper and deeper relationship with our Heavenly Friend. The more we know Him, the more we can trust in his time-transcendent promises.

The next time you face a dire circumstance, remember Frodo and Shelob, sit back, grab the box of popcorn, and say, "God, you've already got this."

Now that's faith.

Chapter 22

THE POWER OF "SECOND BREATH"

Then the Lord God formed a man from the dust of the ground and breathed into his nostrils the breath of life, and the man became a living being.
(Gen. 2:7, NIV)

And with that he breathed on them and said, "Receive the Holy Spirit."
(John 20:22, NIV)

Take a look at the following list of astounding but highly varied feats and ask yourself: What is the single requirement necessary for them all?

- Scaling the top mountain peaks of K2 or Everest
- Shallow-water diving for precious pearls on the ocean floor
- Battling victoriously in a time-extended sword fight
- Performing as an opera singer at Carnegie Hall
- Winning the Tour de France, Boston Marathon or Ironman Triathlon

At first it might appear that athleticism and physical build would be the cohesive link. But most opera singers are not blessed with the musculature of a Tour de France cyclist, nor could they hope to scale Everest. The physical requirements for climbing K2 and the athletic conditioning for sword fighting are considerably varied. Climbers are encouraged to lose weight, where overpowering size might be what tips a sword fight in a warrior's favor.

It cannot be endless years of practice, either. A mere five- or six-year-old child can be a valued pearl diver, but could never compete in the Tour de France, scale Everest or win the Ironman. But there is a single collective requirement necessary for accomplishing all of these amazing escapades. It's not training. It's not athleticism. It's not muscularity or body coordination.

It's breath.

Though we marvel at athleticism and muscularity, and athletes hire strength-conditioning trainers for hundred of dollars per hour, without breath, success in these world-class events would be futile. But it cannot simply be breath alone; each one of us breathes in and out at intervals of three to eight seconds all day, every day. What separates us from all those having accomplished the feats on this list, then, is *breath capacity*. How much breath (or air) your body can hold becomes the critical cohesive factor in whether you can scale mountain peaks; uncover great and priceless underwater treasures; be heralded as victorious in a critical sword battle; or receive the prize and accolades in a contest of endurance, athleticism or vocal prowess.

Looking at the outcomes produced from the list above, it's easy to see how metaphorically positive and potent these actions are. You can view the world from heights only a select few ever see; live in financial prosperity and freedom through the sale of your ocean treasures; win a personal war; or achieve world-renown, acclaim and praise. These are special, rare feats only a very few can claim to have accomplished. And they all require substantial breath capacity to achieve.

Let's get logical for a moment. If these actions all have such strong positive metaphorical and even scriptural support – such as running a race or fighting in person-to-person combat – then would not breath, as the cohesive component to them all, also be spiritually significant? To answer this, we need to understand "breath" scripturally and etymologically. We discover in Genesis that when God created man (Adam) he breathed the breath of life into him. That first natural breath gave mankind the raw resource to achieve all the natural feats cataloged at the beginning of this article. But in the book of Acts, we read that the risen Christ, the new Adam, breathed on His band of uncertain and disjointed disciples to receive the Holy Spirit. The English term "breath" is the Hebrew word "ruach." It is a reference of the term "spirit." It was not just that the disciples had received the Spirit; they had received a second *spiritual* breath, as well.

Jesus said of John – the last of the prophets of natural first breath – that he was the greatest of all those having come before him. But moments later, in Matthew 11:11, Jesus declared that the least in his Kingdom (those with second spiritual breath) were greater than John. Again, Jesus told his disciples that they (only after second breath) would do greater works than even He had done. In fact, Jesus told them to wait in Jerusalem and do nothing – until they had received this second breath. The rest of the book of Acts catalogs the radical feats accomplished after His disciples received second breath. The apostles began to supernaturally heal, raise people from the dead, prophesy about future events with stunning clarity, stave off physical ailments and lead thousands to Christ through minimal sermonettes.

Let's do a natural/supernatural comparison. Is not raising someone from the dead a far greater feat than winning the Tour de France or performing in an opera at Carnegie Hall? Would not someone prefer to be healed of cancer or AIDS than be given a necklace of black pearls and remain in their illness? The second breath is far greater than the first breath, because while the first breath is "human breathed," the second breath is "heaven breathed." Since first breath is "our" breath, its accomplishments are limited to our own physiologic capacity. But second breath is "His" breath. It is a form of breath with accomplishments that have no ceiling! Why? It is not tied to man's physiologic nature. It is tied to God's nature.

So if first breath is the critical link between all these natural, world-renowned successes, and second breath became the conduit for all of the supernatural manifestations in the book of Acts, then why don't we hear about more supernatural phenomena occurring in our culture? Nearly every Christian denomination agrees that a believer receives second breath (the Holy Spirit) at his or her salvation. So what gives?

It may be because second breath also is about capacity.

In the physical, breathing is little more than a natural reflex. The ability to breathe doesn't qualify us to dive for treasures, accomplish great feats of battle, sing in an opera in front of thousands, or scale the heights of the earth. Neither does the mere presence of the Holy Spirit's second breath allow us to accomplish commensurate and surpassing spiritual feats.

As reborn "second breath" Christians, we have the potential for feats greater than any feats in the natural. But our lack of breath capacity has staved off their reality. St. Irenaeus proclaimed, "The glory of God is man fully alive." But instead of being fully alive in great second breath capacity, the church, to many, appears to be somewhat on spiritual life support. So what does that do for God's glory?

Too often we cry out to God for more of His glory, when He's calling out to us to become vessels able to contain what's already available.

The term "revival" often constitutes the desire for something whose dormancy lies outside of mankind. But it is man that is dormant. We don't just need revival. We need repentance. We don't just need more of Him (breath). He needs more of us (capacity). This may sound like some typical church mantra. But Jesus divulged, in exacting detail, His Father's "breath" formula.

It was the Son of God who declared: "And no one puts new wine into old wineskins; or else the new wine will burst the wineskins and be spilled, and the wineskins will be ruined. But new wine must be put into new wineskins, and both are preserved." (Luke 5:37-38, NKJV)

Understanding that the wine in this passage is a metaphor for the Holy Spirit, or the second spiritual breath, and the wineskin is the metaphor for the heart, we can retranslate the passage above to read: "God cannot put greater second breath into a heart unable to handle its capacity. If he does, the new breath will burst the heart. No, second breath must be placed in a heart able to handle its capacity."

Is this a far stretch from Christ's intended meaning? Is there a breath/heart relation to the far superior supernatural acts those with the second breath are to achieve? To answer that question is to go back to our natural breath scenarios. Here again is the list of astounding natural feats:

- Scaling the top mountain peaks of K2 or Everest
- Shallow-water diving for precious pearls on the ocean floor
- Battling victoriously in a time-extended sword fight
- Performing as an opera singer at Carnegie Hall
- Winning the Tour de France, Boston Marathon or Ironman Triathlon

What would happen to an individual attempting to accomplish these astounding natural feats without the proper breath (lung) capacity? Pushing the incapable body to the degree demanded by these actions would produce immense stress on the lungs. Unable to process the amount of air intake necessary, the lungs would start to collapse. The failure of the lungs would cause so much pressure that the natural heart, unable to pump fast enough to remedy the cataclysmic situation, would... burst.

And no one puts new wine into old wineskins; or else the new wine will burst the wineskins....

Our God, the supernatural Creator and Author of our universe and mankind, created a physically observable metaphor that unlocks the secret to our supernatural success. He did not merely say it with His words; he proved it through His crafting of man's own physiology. God made man so that he could not accomplish humanity's most astounding natural feats without first breath capacity just as man cannot accomplish His astounding supernatural feats without second breath capacity. And He made man's heart the central conduit for both. God is exacting in every aspect of the metaphor. Through the natural, He has given us the key (and the warning) to the spiritual.

HOW THEN DO WE LIVE?

As you have already discovered in this book, we increase Breath capacity through ample time in God's word, through an understanding and application of God's ordinances beyond just their moral reasoning, through a healthy and interactive prayer and meditative life, and through an impassioned love for all of those bearing God's image.

God waits on mankind's second breath capacity. He lovingly does not give us the supernatural power we cry out for – which the world desperately needs – if our hearts cannot handle it. Until we, as carriers of eternal life here on earth, build strong enough second breath capacity, the world always is going to revere and honor those with first breath capacity more than us. The astounding feats listed are truly inspiring and life altering. But we were made for supernatural feats far surpassing those on the natural list the moment we were given the spiritual breath to accomplish them.

I can do all things through Christ who (whose breath) strengthens me. (Phil. 4:13, NKJV, parentheses added)

"All things" means every spiritual height, every spiritual treasure, every spiritual battle, every spiritual prize and accolade. It's not some fantastical pipe dream. It's His plan. What's required is capacity.

Chapter 23

ELEVENTH-HOUR EVANGELISM

Ponder:

For the kingdom of heaven is like a landowner who went out early in the morning to hire laborers for his vineyard. When he had agreed with the laborers for a denarius for the day, he sent them into his vineyard. And he went out about the third hour... and said, 'You also go into the vineyard and whatever is right I will give you.'... Again, he went out about the sixth and the ninth hour, and did the same thing. And about the eleventh hour he went out and found others standing around; and he said to them, 'Why have you been standing here idle all day long?' They said to him, 'Because no one hired us.' He said to them, 'You go into the vineyard too.'"
(Matt. 20: 1- 7, NASB; read Matt 20: 1-16)

Much of today's church is clamoring for cultural relevancy. Christian leadership conferences, evangelistic books and Christian-radio talk show hosts all are debating how to be more "relevant" to an ever-growing, post-modern culture. Churches bait the lost souls of the X, Y and millennial generations with MTV-style visuals and worship, iPad or Wii giveaways, entertainment-based preaching and constant references to social networks and the latest movie or cable television show. All in the hopes that through these media and tactics people will somehow see and recognize the need for God's Kingdom.

Sadly, the current culture recognizes the inconsistencies. According to *unChristian*, when polled, the vast majority of America's young people claimed the church is "judgmental" (87 percent); "hypocritical" (85 percent); and "old-fashioned" (78 percent) (p. 27)[1]. And in just three years, 2003-2006, the percentage of adults that were "absolutely certain" there even is a God dropped a staggering 12 percent[2]. Despite a multi-decade crusade for "relevance," society is growing perpetually less tolerant and considerate of America's current form of Christianity.

But it is not cultural relevance that will bridge the growing gap between our current society and the church. *It's cultural engagement.*

From the central point of view, the spotlight of the parable at the beginning of this chapter appears to focus on the amount of work each group completed contrasted with their equal pay at the end of the day. As if affirming this central lesson, the parable ends (except in the King James and New King James versions) with Jesus asserting that the "last shall be first, and the first last." For years, I heard numerous sermons giving me solace that should I have an alcoholic, philandering, God-hating distant relative, his or her death-bed repentance meant the same salvation as someone like my grandfather, a multi-decade, self-styled missionary and builder of countless churches in other nations. But extending the camera lens back a little wider, a far more universal and historically relevant finding is uncovered. From that lens we will unpack what I am calling eleventh-hour evangelism; uncover its critical historical need; address its (currently) counter-intuitive approach; and expose the honorable and humbling position this group has been given.

A VERY UNIQUE HOUR

Based on the limited information in this passage, we first find a central character (a landowner) and an opportunity (working in his vineyard). But any opportunity needs capable fulfillers. So the landowner travels to the marketplace to do his recruiting. In the early morning, he hires the passage's most skilled negotiators and sends them into his vineyard. Though wage is not specifically discussed, he offers a similar opportunity to those standing in the marketplace on the third, sixth, ninth and eleventh hours. As the workday concludes, the men, some more exhausted than others, line up for compensation. To the surprise of the early-hour workers, each group receives the same wage. Thus we clearly are shown and then even told that the first and the last were on equal footing; case dismissed, lesson learned.

But shifting the focus toward the periphery of the story, something very unique happens in the eleventh hour. The eleventh-hour group didn't just head out into the vineyard. *They had to be engaged.* The previous four groups heard the offer, recognized some form of compensation, and went. But for the eleventh-hour group, employment called for a new method. *The eleventh hour required interactive dialogue.*

CULTURAL ENGAGEMENT

Eschatology aside, I believe that we are living in an eleventh-hour society. In response, it is time for a new paradigm in evangelism. What saved us, whether in the first, third, sixth or ninth hour, won't have the same impact on this eleventh-hour society. It is not merely new first- to ninth-hour evangelism tactics, but a new methodology of evangelism that should be explored. Its genesis is a radical paradigm shift from "cultural relevance" to "cultural engagement."

ELEVENTH-HOUR ASPECTS AND APPLICATION

"… [A]nd about the eleventh hour he went and found others standing around…."

ASPECT 1: The eleventh-hour group had been standing in the same marketplace as the previous four groups. The eleventh-hour group was not disconnected from the previous four groups. They were an essential part of the equation.

ELEVENTH-HOUR APPLICATION: The church must recognize that despite ideological bias, deviant behavior or gross character flaw, every individual is first and foremost made in the image of God. One of the problems with our past forms of evangelism is that we see non-Christians as "sinners" first, rather than as unique and infinitely special images of God. While the church recognizes itself as God's children, it fails to see the large portions of humanity as God's creations. Good-intended Christians often look down on those unable to break addictive habits; those engaged in deviant actions; or those with ideological or gender preferences other than their own. We rarely see the pain of an individual's past story over the moral misbehavior of the moment. Our banner-waving animosity toward certain groups of humanity specifically, and even intentionally, strips them of their "image of God" heritage. This is a gross failure. To see any one of God's images with disgust, disdain or hatred is actually to view them through satanic lenses. It is the devil that hates humanity, and by taking any such attitude, regardless of whatever ideological, moral or character flaws any person may have, we actually partner with his agenda.

The eleventh-hour evangelism method is not to condone "sinful" behavior, but to understand it tactically as a strategy against individuals and ultimately humanity. It is recognizing the difference between identity and actions. Ideology, religion or even claimed sexual preference does not determine one's identity. It merely helps to affect and shape one's actions. Everyone is made in the image of God. But actions produce consequences often harmful to the individual, the generations, and the society, stripping away at the soul and spirit, often through the destruction of the body. By empathetically acknowledging how particular actions, and specifically their consequence, play out on humanity, shifts the church's reaction to "sins" from moral superiority to concern for the well-being of humanity. The church's focus in this eleventh hour should be the evidential damage caused to those made in God's image, not merely the immoral damage caused by sinners. A recent Barna poll showed the leading concern among modern evangelicals was the need for stronger moral value in America. But until the church recognizes why God established certain moral or dogmatic boundaries, it is merely driving a deeper wedge between itself and the eleventh-hour society. Because that is not how the landowner engaged...

"...[A]nd he said to them, 'Why have you been standing here idle all day long?'"

ASPECT 2: Eleventh-hour conversation began with selfless, inquisitive interaction. The beginning of the eleventh-hour dialogue began with a question motivated not out of control, but out of concern: 'Why are you still here? What is it about this message that hasn't drawn you yet?" The modern church holds numerous summits and roundtables in search of the best tactics to "win" or "entertain" people into its doors. From multimedia presentations, to outside fairs and festivals and even extreme sports expositions, the church attempts to bring in the disinterested masses, only to "bait and switch" attendees into hearing about what they are missing. Instead, the church should be asking society: "What are _we_ missing?"

ELEVENTH-HOUR APPLICATION: The church must shift its evangelistic approach from speaking to listening and acting. Instead of preaching at "the lost," the church must engage God's image first. It must meet the eleventh-hour group at its point of need; first finding out what those needs are and then partnering with the group to see those needs addressed. Because of the church's apparent disconnect with this eleventh-hour society, it should not be surprised that the first dialogue of needs may not be soul level. But the eleventh-hour group is looking for alleviation to situations that are, by default (and by intent), harming the soul. Through self-centered, pleasure-first methodologies and advertising, isolative technologies, and impersonal ideologies, the eleventh-hour populous has erected powerful self-sufficient barricades choking out the value and need of the soul. But in doing so, it is decimating the body and the mind. Currently more than 36 million

Americans suffer from some form of mental disorder or fear; 25 percent of the populous has some form of venereal disease; one in four women has been raped or molested; cancer and diabetes wrack humanity; addiction in a myriad of forms is a staple of society; and poverty and indebtedness plague multi-millions.

Our eleventh-hour society is looking for those who can address issues such as these. How can we be so sure? They are flocking *en masse* to the false saviors of pharmacology, entertainment, government, and co-opted mysticism. Because of the church's growing pharisaical nature, the eleventh-hour group may not currently want anything to do with the Christian's God. But they are desperate to rid themselves of the consequences of a godless society. Our relativistic society propagates its actions through the subjective mantra, "I can do anything I want." But it loathes the damaging objective consequence it cannot control. And it will go anywhere it can to get relief without judgmentalism. Which leads to the next aspect:

"He said to them, 'You go into the vineyard too.'"
ASPECT 3: The landowner recognized the eleventh-hour group's personal sense of self-satisfaction, but was certain he could offer something better. When the landowner speaks to the eleventh-hour group, he asks them, "Why have you been standing here idle all day?" The word "standing" is the Hebrew term 'Histemi;' its definition includes "standing firm, continued safe and sound, of quality" and "unhesitating." The eleventh-hour group personally considered standing unemployed in the marketplace beneficial to them. The landowner first and foremost recognizes their personal sense of self-satisfaction and security.

But he also is fully confident in his own offer. The Hebrew term for "idle" is "argos," which translates as "careless, useless or lazy." After acknowledging their perception of their market place idleness as "of quality and secure," he tells them that in reality it has been useless. Such a bold declaration requires absolute certainty in his particular offer and leads to a two-tiered application.

ELEVENTH-HOUR APPLICATION 1: The church's failure to engage culture at its place of need has produced highly enjoyable and holistically satisfying technological and ideological competition. Because of the supposed lackluster evidence of the church's "saltiness," the world has become a haven for comfort, ease and technological dependence. This book repeatedly exposes its outcome as cataclysmic. But in the immediate moment, the world's offers are engaging, enjoyable and sufficient enough for the comfort and ease of the average citizen. We now face a citizenry dependent on outside mechanisms for daily function and interaction. Americans watch 8.1 hours of television per day, spend countless hours in social networks, couldn't think of living without tablets or smart phones, and spend whatever waking moments they can in virtual worlds like *Second Life*. Regardless of the implications, society has grown comfortable in that state. It is merely a part of the backsplash of modern life. The world doesn't feel it is missing anything, and in fact turns the tables on the church. Like Pilgrim experienced in his venture through Vanity Fair, the world considers the Christian to be the one missing out on all life has to offer. Which is where the second discovery leads us.

ELEVENTH-HOUR APPLICATION 2: Despite scriptural assurance that Christianity is the best way of living, the church's evidence is grossly lacking. The church, as a universal body of believers, hasn't failed society. But church members, inept at living life with more zeal, richness, depth, compassion and insight than the average non-believer, can soil the power of the gospel. According to much of the culture, the church is grossly failing at living a "taste and see" evidential lifestyle. Instead, it is content to criticize others for what they place in their mouths. The church must live a Kingdom-focused life capable of producing such powerful evidence of Christ's love and the Spirit's wisdom that it silences every anti-Christian ambassador. The church must live the gospel, not merely preach it. Preaching requires no evidence of its claims. The eleventh-hour society, rife with a myriad of subjective voices, is looking for proof, not petitions. Megachurches and expository preachers may flourish if their sanctuaries are stacked with the first- through ninth-hour groups. But without verifiable, transformative evidence, the church may have fewer and fewer inroads into this eleventh-hour society.

"They said to him, 'Because no one hired us.'"
ASPECT 4: Nothing said prior resonated with the eleventh-hour group. Scripture makes it clear that the group also had been "standing all day" in the same marketplace. But under questioning, the eleventh-hour response was, "No one has hired us." Nothing in the previous four petitions resonated with this group. It wasn't necessarily that they were adverse to employment at the vineyard; it was that they had felt no draw from all previous methods of solicitation.

ELEVENTH-HOUR APPLICATION: The church must not merely uncover and address societal needs; it must speak through the culture's various voices. The eleventh-hour society is not looking for the church to repackage its evangelistic message in their language. The eleventh-hour society isn't even looking for the church. But if "all truth is God's truth," then scriptural truth can be spoken and validated in the language of the domain in which it is applied. The church must avoid simply adopting culture to promote the gospel, but use the holistic Biblical Worldview to objectively explain, uncover and remedy culture's most troubling issues and concerns. It is not merely theology, but biblical wisdom and understanding, that will be the foundational starting point for solutions in all of society's many and broad domains. In a culture that has distanced itself from its Creator, the best its experts can offer is knowledge, which is rarely capable of transcending its particular sphere of application (experts in law often cannot speak into another domain, such as neuroscience). Wisdom, as a transcending and transformative force, becomes the lens through which knowledge is filtered, as you will discover in Chapter 25.

It may be that the world will pay more attention to the church when, through wisdom and understanding, it can better explain and apply the findings and discoveries of society's many domains than any of its previous secular, knowledge-based experts. But the church was never meant to do this alone. The church must recognize the holistic and transcendent power of wisdom and develop strategic relationships with society's experts in knowledge. This "paradigm of partnership" between experts in knowledge and leaders in wisdom will ensure the church won't dominate culture. Instead, it will help shape it. Through the correct understanding and application of knowledge, wisdom and understanding (Chapter 25), the church will become the forerunner to solving the world's most complex problems - in its own languages. It will rebuild the "ancient ruins" and by default become "the city on a hill" it always was meant to be. But it must do so with the utmost sense of previous regret and present humility.

"They said to him, 'Because no one hired us.' He said to them, 'You go into the vineyard too.'"

ASPECT 5: Of the five groups of laborers, the eleventh-hour was the pinnacle of humility and selflessness. While the other groups were promised some form of compensation, the eleventh-hour group (once engaged) went without negotiation or future incentive. They required no outlandish proposition, merely engaging dialog.

ELEVENTH-HOUR APPLICATION: The church must recognize its moral superiority complex may be both the world's – and God's – greatest turnoff. Christians tend to see themselves as superior: morally, philosophically and spiritually. But despite our promised heritage as the principal purveyors of "truth," our superiority complex may actually turn God off. When the eleventh-hour group receives the same compensation as the first hour (one denarius), the first hour grumbles and complains. To this, the landowner refers to the first-hour laborers as "evil." Now wait a minute. The first-hour laborers had borne the brunt of burden in the "scorching heat" of the day. But the landowner still calls them evil. Why? Their focus was internal and narcissistic, instead of external and selfless.

Their argument for greater compensation was rooted in their own needs and based on their own previous accomplishments. But there was another way for the first-hour group to view their position: that of their value of service to the landowner and his customers. The first hour was given the high honor of providing the most benefit to the landowner. His customers received the greatest fruit from the first-hour group's labor. But instead of relishing in their altruism, they remained egocentric. The attitude of the first-hour laborers reflected, in part, their perceived value of the landowner and his customers. We can see this same understanding through the older son in the Prodigal story. We must keep our hearts and minds focused on Christ and our able hands and loving eyes on the people around us.

ASPECT 6: The eleventh-hour group's aversion and hatred of Christians is due to the fact that our failures have lead to the consequences they must now endure. Because the church has, at times, been internally focused, elitist, judgmental and morally driven, the world wants little to do with Christianity, apart from an open hand during environmental disasters or the occasional bandage when times get personally trying. Scripturally, we are assured that when the world acts "worldly," it is operating inside its own nature. To blame the world for acting inside its own inherency is like attacking a lion for being a carnivore. Instead, the church should humbly and compassionately recognize that because of our failures, society's lions are now feeding on their own flesh for sustenance and satisfaction. The world is desperate for pleasure, but it is helpless when it comes to the consequence of those actions.

The role of the church, regardless of its first/ninth hour failure, is to display a reality so wonderfully fruitful, so radically winsome, that the world intentionally changes its harmful-yet-pleasurable direction and follows a different course. Our own failures have given full access to the intent of worldliness: death, destruction and misery. Worldly actions are part and parcel with unsaved humanity. Damaging Consequence, however, is not God's intended intent for His image. But both come hand in hand. The failure of the church to fully remain "salt and light" has led to the gross destruction of much of the rest of humanity. The church, to much of the culture, remains morally elitist while the world still embraces sin's pleasurable intent. And neither side recognizes worldly action for its strategic consequence. But if we are honest, the blame should tip further toward the church, for its failure to act according to its intended nature, has led the eleventh-hour society to rush head-first into its destructive inherency.

The eleventh-hour group isn't strictly looking for compensation for itself. Its concerned focus is on alleviation for its fellow man, the environment and other affective issues. It has been riddled with the consequence brought about by our lack of evidence and hypocrisy, and it wants to see something done about it. Instead of launching attacks or boycotts, the church must first recognize its own failures, humbly admit to its primary role in the degradation of society, and begin to partner with the eleventh-hour cohort for positive transformative change.

ASPECT 7: All other groups were called, but the eleventh-hour group specifically was chosen. All other groups were presented an offer and either took it or negotiated for the best terms. But the eleventh-hour group appears to be special; it was given equal standing; the statement is that the "last shall be first."

ELEVENTH-HOUR APPLICATION: Despite their look, attitude, character and temperament, the church must recognize that the currently unsaved just might be God's greatest treasures. We may have come into His fold in the earlier hours, but it may have been for the purpose of the group that currently wants little to do with the church. There must be a radical humility from the currently saved to those of the eleventh hour. Our arms must be open and accepting; our posture must be that of support rather than just instruction; our voice must resonate into the culture; and our fruit must be by far the most delicious on earth. Should we continue to attempt first-, third-, sixth- or ninth-hour evangelism, our solicitations may fail both humanity and the God who has chosen this group for His special purposes.

IN CONCLUSION

Eleventh-hour evangelism is not the preaching of a watered-down gospel. It is swallowing the holistic Biblical Worldview whole and allowing people to see the gospel's power through the visage of transformed individuals and eventually, communities and nations. It sees all people as images of God, not select people as numbers for a church or denomination. And most importantly, it operates under the radical presupposition that if applied correctly, the gospel will cause all arenas of human existence to be holistically transformed in far greater measure than its current experts claim possible. It doesn't wait for the future Kingdom, but attempts to bring the Kingdom to earth. It believes that man should first be made "fully alive" so then he (and the rest of the world) can then see the "glory of God." It recognizes the weight of its current responsibility and past failure to this eleventh-hour society while also fully grasping the power of its own offer. In other words, while the believer comes to God as a son and joint-heir, he comes to the eleventh-hour society as a servant.

1. Kinnaman, David, and Gabe Lyons, *unChristian*, Grand Rapids: Baker Books, 2007. Print.

2. The Harris Poll(R) #80, October 31, 2006

Chapter 24

ILLUMI**NATION**: THE POWER (OR WEAKNESS) OF CHRISTIAN LIGHT

Ponder:
This is the message we have heard from him and declare to you: God is <u>light</u>; in him there is no darkness at all.
(1 John 1:5 NIV, underline mine)

A number of years ago, a colleague of mine and I took this verse to literal heart. Our thought was that if God is "light" as the verse above states, then we should be able to understand more about God through a deeper understanding of light. So we brought a lighting expert into our office. His task was to sit with us for one hour and dialog about his vocational field. We had no idea what we'd discover, we simply prayed for divine inspiration and took copious notes. Within 20 minutes, we had 'laser' clarity as to why the church has lost so much impact in our culture and why the gay movement in America is such a powerful force today...

This particular expert specialized in light dynamics for concerts and events. His work entailed using lasers to produce dazzling visual spectacles for some of music's biggest stars. Lasers are powerful beams of focused light that, depending on their optical strength, can cut holes through just about anything. But in his field, visual spectacles with light requires "splitting" the beam into multiple light sources and then redirecting those beams to dazzle and amaze concert-goers.

But once a laser is fractured into multiple beams it loses optical power. Or, we could say, it loses its intended impact. Though it may entertain, its power as a cutting force diminishes every time the light is reflected or refracted. Take a laser that can bore through solid metal and split in a few times and you can run your hand over the new beam without even feeling a tickle. And in that understanding, a new "light" dawned...

God is light, pure and powerful holiness, love and truth. Like a laser, scripture asserts that God's Word is able to separate soul and spirit, joint and marrow (Heb. 4:12). As his ambassadors, we most often carry and disseminate that Light through our churches. But, like a laser splitter, our pure light has grown fractured. It happens through denominational segmentations, it happens through church splits, it happens through our mistrust in churches that don't look or act like our particular stream. We judge each other based on our political stances, our eschatological viewpoints, our evangelistic techniques, our forms of worship or our acceptance or rejection of various segments of society. And in most cities, instead of cohesion, we find fragmentation. And in the eyes of the general populous, each act of refraction reduces the "purity" and "potency" of our message.

As the church, we are God's mechanism of Light transmission. But instead of bringing together the Light, we split it in a million directions, reduce its focal power and then wonder why we aren't making more of an impact on our culture.

Which brings us to the gay movement.

Like a precise and purposed laser, the gay movement has its own agenda and its aim is the minds and hearts of the culture at large. But instead of splitting off its light with infighting, exclusion or separate desires, everything is brought back to a focal center. It doesn't matter what your beliefs, what your background is, what your political stance may be or how you worship or don't worship, if you are gay you are supported by your community. Instead of outward backbiting and mistrust, there appears, at least on the surface, to be acceptance and inclusion. Focally, there is little refraction. It is a community 'laser' fused with purpose, acceptance and openness.

Both at the city AND the national level, that is what the culture sees. Their "light" is cutting through every domain of society and gaining considerable traction every day. And when the fractured beams of the true Light attack the laser precision focus and acceptance of the gay movement, the culture at large screams "hypocrisy" and/or "intolerance," and our focal power continues to diminish. If you think that seems too extreme, consider what our culture now considers "controversial." Is it them? Or is it us...

The answer is not to continue our futile attempt to dismantle their laser. The answer is to fix ours. We must come together in unity, mutual respect and love. We must recognize that no one church has all the answers. We are a wonderfully diverse body of congregations with Christ as the focal head. Scripturally, God works through cities, and the populous of a city must see a unified movement, not a disparate smattering of churches rarely willing to reach out to one another or support each other's missions. For us to make a tangible difference in our cities the populous must not see refracted denominations; they must see true, pure and unadulterated Light.

SO WHAT NOW?

Here is a vision I have been sharing with pastors and leaders that I am blessed to call friends. Imagine if a city of Christ-centered churches came together, first in prayer and fellowship and then in mission. They began by getting to know one another, holding citywide church leadership luncheons and prayer meetings available to all denominations. And then, as relationships develop, those leaders intentionally tackled a citywide mission; say poverty, addiction, homelessness, etc. And they branded their mission, with "were working on it." Imagine a city full of billboards like the following:

For one year, the entire city of churches came together over one mission, hosting prayer meetings, coordinating messages, creating interdenominational events and outreaches, working with governmental leadership, the arts, and other domains, all with a central "laser focused" purpose. At the end of the year, the tangible impact of that mission would be documented and the findings presented to the culture through its media channels and educational systems. And the next year, a new mission would be adopted.

Imagine if this didn't just take place over a city, but over cities, throughout this entire great nation. As the church, our light may now be refracted; but if and when we come together, we have the answers for this hurting world. We have been given the solutions for their bodies, minds, as well as their souls. Let us recognize our own refraction and once again fuse the true Light of the world by unifying our "body" and lovingly addressing our cities' areas of darkness together.

You are the light of the world. A city set on a hill cannot be hidden (Matthew 5:14 NASB, emphasis mine)

Chapter 25

A HIGH CALL TO MEN AND WOMEN OF UNDERSTANDING

Ponder:
Those who have insight will shine brightly like the brightness of the expanse of heaven, and those who lead many to righteousness, like the stars forever and ever.
(Dan. 12:3, NASB)

We are nearing the end of this book. I hope these chapters have inspired you, challenged you and presented you with a faith far bigger and more relevant (or resonant) than you may ever have realized. In that realization you have discovered whom you are fighting for (humanity); whom you are fighting against (the enemy and his tactics); and whom you are fighting with (God, His Son and Spirit, and with other believers). You have been shown a new way to communicate with others and to address society's ills and confusion, and been given tools to see your communication and intimacy with your Creator flourish. In this chapter I'd like to talk to you specifically. For I believe that if you have read this book, whether you purchased it yourself, or were given the book by a friend, you feel a call and a pull to something more powerful and potent than just a Sunday morning Christianity. If you are like many I have talked to, you probably haven't been able to fully express your passions or desires for God's Kingdom, but I am hopeful that this chapter puts words to the desires of your heart.

I believe that if you are reading this book, your burning desire is to become a *man or woman of understanding*.

To understand the magnitude of that last sentence, we need to break down three seemingly synonymous terms: wisdom, knowledge and understanding. On the surface, they seem to be used interchangeably, but through a deeper mining of the book of Proverbs the powerful differences between these three words emerge. And in that emergence, a call rings out.

CLASSIFICATION 1: WISDOM

There have been many hypotheses over the definition of the term "wisdom." I've often heard leaders declare: "Wisdom is knowledge applied." More recently, I caught a sermon defining wisdom as "having the ability to make right choices where the moral rules don't apply." Although these may be decent explanations of the word, and each certainly has merit, neither definition accounts for the incalculable value bestowed on wisdom through the biblical text:

If you seek her as silver And search for her as for hidden treasures. (Prov. 2:4, NASB)

She is more precious than jewels; And nothing you desire compares with her. (Prov. 3:15, NASB)

Thankfully, the Bible uncovers key qualifications and attributes of wisdom, and in the process unveils its immense holistic and transforming value:

In Proverbs 8 we are given a *historical* account of wisdom:

The Lord possessed me at the beginning of His way, Before His works of old. From everlasting I was established, From the beginning, from the earliest times of the earth.... When He set for the sea its boundary, So that water would not transgress His command, When he marked out the foundations of the earth; Then I was beside Him, as a master workman; And I was daily His delight, Rejoicing always before Him.... (Prov. 8:22-23, 29-30, NASB)

Through this poetic monologue, a finely contiguous and nearly hidden secret is unearthed: Wisdom existed PRE-FALL. The passage above states that wisdom was established, from the earliest times of the earth; it was the Master Workman at its creation. Wisdom did not merely fashion the earth; it fashioned the earth in its perfect state. The next passage not only echoes this realization; it adds even greater significance to the term. For wisdom was there:

While He had not yet made the earth and the fields, Nor the first dust of the world. (Prov. 8:26, NASB, underline added)

Why is this passage so critically important? Because, according to the Bible, God made man from dust. If there was no dust, then logically there was no man. So here we learn that wisdom not only existed pre-man, but she (described metaphorically in the feminine) helped fashion mankind: "Rejoicing in the world, His earth, and having my delight in the sons of men." (Prov. 8:31, NASB) So once again, wisdom did not merely help assist in the creation of mankind; wisdom formulated mankind in his pre-fall, and therefore, also-perfect state. This passage in Proverbs reveals just how powerful and precious wisdom actually is; it is not merely "knowledge applied" or a "right choice" outside of an obvious moral distinction. Instead:

Wisdom is culmination of the foundational laws, principals and regulations governing all fields of natural existence and humanity in their perfect, pre-fall state.

We now can grasp why wisdom is declared to be more valuable than gold and silver, why we must seek it above jewels and search for it as buried treasure. If wisdom constitutes the principles required for perfection across all fields of existence, then it is something impossible to buy at any price. For the world (as we now understand), operating in a post-fall state, does not have it to offer. This also solidifies why God would grant wisdom to "anyone who asks." Because it is the Creator's blueprint for His original and always-intended agenda: *"There I was a master workman, and I was daily His delight."* (Proverbs 8:30 NASB) In Proverbs, we also learn another distinction for this blueprint; it is referred to as His "way." The same passage states that: *"The Lord possessed me at the beginning of His way, Before his works of old."* (Proverbs 8:22 NASB) What works? The creation of the world: *"from the beginning, from the earliest times of the earth."* (Proverbs 8:23 NASB)

Or, the creation of the world in its perfect, pre-fall state.

We can take this understanding to the wisest man ever to exist, the man who penned the very wisdom literature referenced here. Solomon, in his famous petition, did not appeal to God for the mere wisdom of man, such as the vast intelligence of men like Plato, Socrates and Aristotle. Instead, it appears his request was to be given the principles through which the earth was created pre-fall. We discover the reality of this principle in Solomon's famous prayer. *"So give your servant an understanding heart to judge your people to discern (understand) between good and evil."* (I Kings 3:9 NASB, parenthesis mine)

CLASSIFICATON 2: (THE TURN TOWARD) KNOWLEDGE

This is a very interesting turn of phrase; for it bears a slight familiarity with another passage found far earlier in the Bible. In fact, it was a pre-fall declaration by the Creator of the perfect world: *"but from the tree of the knowledge of good and evil you shall not eat, for in the day that you eat from it you shall surely die."* (Genesis 2:17 NASB) Here we see something even more profound and through it we can unlock just how our first two terms are tangibly separated. The scriptures have already shown that wisdom was in the garden of God and that wisdom existed and is ordered pre-fall. But in Genesis 3 we discover that mankind rejected wisdom. That rejection manifested through the eating of the particular tree they were forbidden to eat from. And what did mankind eat? Knowledge.

[B]ut from the tree of the knowledge of good and evil.... (Gen. 2:17, NASB)

Mankind rejected wisdom and instead chose the *knowledge* of good and evil. And therein lies the difference between the first two distinctions: Wisdom is a pre-fall entity; but knowledge is POST-FALL. Wisdom dominated and operated the world's systems in perfection *until* mankind chose to reject wisdom and instead chose knowledge. Therefore, a new definition for knowledge can now be added:

Wisdom: The foundational laws, principals and regulations that govern all fields of existence and humanity in their perfect, pre-fall state.

Knowledge: Any single discovery of the new systems, principals and regulations of the earth and/or mankind now existing post-fall, or outside of their originally created context.

We now can determine the outcome of both of these entities. Wisdom produces perfection, since it is pre-fall. But knowledge, taken wholly on its own, produces destruction, since it is a post-fall entity and now operating under the law of sin and entropy. Again, the Bible appears to show this to be the case: *"For he who finds me (wisdom) finds life, And obtains favor from the LORD. But he who sins against me (misses the mark of wisdom) injures himself; All those who hate me (wisdom) love death.* "(Prov. 8:35, NASB, parentheses added)

Since wisdom comes from the Creator of the earth, mankind and the universe, the rejection and deliberate removal of the Creator carries far deeper consequence; it's also a rejection of wisdom; a dismissal of the pre-fall principles of the earth; and an embrace of a post-fall, entropy-centric earth. Listen to wisdom's call through this lens: *"They would not accept my counsel, they spurned all my reproof. So they shall eat the fruit of their own way, and be satiated with their own devices. For the waywardness of the naïve will kill them, and the complacency of fools will destroy them."* (Prov. 1:30-32, NASB) The further mankind moves away from its Creator, the further mankind must, by default, move away from wisdom, and the more inevitable the destruction on the creation. As non-theist leaders have distanced mankind from a supposed arcane and irrelevant Deity, they actually have removed mankind from its own perfection and protection. Listen to the Creator's petition to those reveling in their post-fall state and deliberately rejecting the Lord: *"Do they spite Me?" declares the LORD. "Is it not themselves they spite, to their own shame?"* (Jer. 7:19, NASB)

IN THE (SECOND) BEGINNING...

It is then possible to track precisely when and how the beginnings of this secular divergence occurred. Secular modern philosophy hinges on the foundational tenet "Cogito Ergo Sum," or "I think, therefore I am." It is from this point the "study of thought" diverged from its prior state as Pope John Paul II declared:

> *The cogito, ergo sum (I think, therefore I am) radically changed the way of doing philosophy. In the pre-Cartesian period, philosophy, that is to say the cogito, or rather the cognosco was subordinate to the esse... To Descartes, however, the esse seemed secondary, and he judged the cogito to be prior... After Descartes, philosophy became a science of pure thought... both the created world and the Creator—remained within the cogito as the content of human consciousness. Philosophy now concerned itself with beings qua content of consciousness and not qua existing independently of it. (Memory and Identity, pp 8-9)*

But exploring this epochal moment through the lens of this wisdom/knowledge paradigm, a far greater revelation unfolds. Descartes' declaration can be amplified to: "I have the capacity to produce and comprehend knowledge ("I think"), and therefore that revelation becomes the central point to my existence ("I am.")" The roads of these two worldviews now diverge in nearly exactly opposite directions.

At the beginning of creation, God said, "Let there be light," and created the world through wisdom (pre-fall perfection).

Whereas:

At the Enlightenment, secular man said, "Let there be light," and began   <u>recreating</u>   the   world   through   knowledge   (post-fall entropy/destruction).

The centuries having passed since Descartes' declaration have been littered with non-theistic, secular leaders, <u>inadvertently</u> recreating the world through knowledge. As citizens bound to the early part of this 21st century, we have been handed a world in which knowledge is used to formulate new knowledge, and so on and so forth. Like a photocopy repeatedly switched out and re-copied again and again, each new generational image becomes a further and further distortion of its once-perfect and protected original image. Inside this distortion, society now functions. Inside this distortion, society now adjudicates. Inside this distortion, society now parents and educates. Inside this distortion, society's institutions now anemically perpetuate. Inside this distortion, society's diversionary technologies and systems are birthed.

This is not simply a moral distortion, as many religious leaders seem to hypothesize. For if knowledge, on its own, carries at its root core and application post-fall entropy and destruction, the more mankind embraces knowledge and rejects wisdom the more post-fall entropy and destruction permeate both the societal and the physical landscape.

Not just its religious/spiritual state.

We now live in a paradox. The world and humanity were created PRE-FALL but eventually were thrust into a POST-FALL existence. But as we learned in previous chapters, God still desired humanity to live its best pre-fall life inside of a post-fall world. So any objective solution to that end must be a bridge between both wisdom (pre-fall) and knowledge (post-fall), since mankind and the universe is now a combination of both.

CLASSIFICATION 3: (THE KEY TO) "UNDERSTANDING"

This bridge is found through the last of the three supposedly synonymous terms: "understanding." In a moment, I will objectively uncover exactly how the secular world remains incapable of producing understanding, and how the church, through the creation of its own form of moralistic dualism, can likewise neither utilize its power. But first, I will use the biblical text to unlock the code to "understanding."

The beginning of wisdom is: Acquire wisdom; And with all your acquiring, get understanding. (Prov. 4:7 NASB)

But knowledge is easy to one who has understanding. (Prov. 14:6b NASB)

By wisdom a house is built, And by understanding it is established; And by knowledge the rooms are filled, With all precious and pleasant riches." (Prov. 24: 3-4, NASB)

Based on these verses, we can deduce: Understanding is acquired through wisdom; easily uncovers knowledge; and acts as the establishment between wisdom and knowledge. Therefore, a rational formula for "understanding" can now be developed:

Knowledge (a discovery of facets of post-fall existence) FILTERED through wisdom (God's divine pre-fall order to existence) PRODUCES understanding.

Understanding operates inside both realms of existence, pre-fall *and* post-fall. Understanding takes any portion of knowledge (post-fall) and filters it through wisdom (pre-fall), producing the most optimal state in our post-fall world for any particular post-fall element of existence. Understanding uncovers that knowledge is not ultimate "power" as Sir Francis Bacon claimed. Knowledge is merely a subset, and subordinate, to wisdom. Salvation and sanctification notwithstanding, wisdom is one of the foremost important entities in post-fall existence, and the initial catalyst for producing understanding. And therefore understanding – knowledge filtered through wisdom – has the capacity to transform culture, just as "knowledge-upon-knowledge" will distort, if not destroy it, and "wisdom-upon-wisdom" produces elitism and humanitarian negligence:

By the transgression of a land many are its princes, But by a man of understanding and knowledge, so it endures. (Prov. 28:2 NASB)

Man in his pomp, yet without understanding, is like the beasts that perish. (Ps. 49:20, NASB)

If we wanted to market the term, we could say that understanding is:

<u>Strategies of heaven that transform earth.</u>

Were God, and thereby Jesus, merely man's Savior, His call might have been: "Come out of this world and be separate." But because God also is Creator, Jesus' mission becomes far more engaging: "Go back into this world and <u>transform</u> it." Not merely with theology, moral values or even solely salvation, but also through understanding; taking the wisdom of the Creator and applying it like a pre-fall salve to all creation in its fallen and flawed state, displaying both God and His love for His creation simultaneously. This is a crucial part of His "way," that "ministry of reconciliation" spoken about in earlier chapters. We then can affix a slight addendum to the statement above: Understanding then becomes…

Strategies of heaven that transform earth *back to its intended state*.

Or using scripture…

[Y]our kingdom come, your will be done, on earth as it is in heaven. (Matt. 6:10, NIV)

THE CALL IS GOING OUT

This chapter has been designed to create a resonance with those that now feel this pull toward being men and women of understanding. For many, it has been impossible to put to words. It exists as a feeling that they are called to help God put this world back "to rights" as N.T. Wright would say. I believe that the "days" Daniel described in this chapter's opening verse are unfolding now, and men and women of understanding will soon accomplish far more than centuries of past leaders ever dreamed possible and incalculably overshadow the tragic aftermath of man's somewhat understandable embrace of the knowledge-upon-knowledge paradigm.

I believe that across America and the world, men and women of understanding eagerly are germinating and being trained and "renewed" by the Spirit, and are ready to pierce the fallaciously indestructible walls of non-belief with undiscovered biblical wisdom and truth applicable to all of humanity. But because there are few "transforming" outlets inside our often morally-dependent church culture, such individuals have remained primarily dormant, content to keep their revelations in personal journals or spoken among the few who will listen to their discoveries without the eye of skepticism. In many cases I was one of that throng.

It is not that their "understanding" should be met with skepticism, for this "knowledge filtered through wisdom produces understanding" discovery is a direct and spiritual component of the Biblical Worldview. Instead, because few extract the Biblical Worldview outside of its own field – moral teaching, daily principled living and future (but wondrous) promises – those that would proclaim such critical understandings are forced to remain silent and on the fringe. They are voracious consumers of the Word of God, because that is the language of our Creator and our pre-fall earth. But they also are tireless devourers of science, law, philosophy, psychology and the humanities, because they also understand our post-fall environment. And they have endured, like the biblical Daniel, not having sold out to a post-fall (knowledge-on-knowledge) world system but instead embracing their pre-fall Creator and His tenets. I believe that this remnant will be given tools and strategies that will cause individuals, governments and nations to marvel.

I believe that if men and women of understanding are developed and given a voice, they have the capacity to transform entire societies, not just congregations. They do not in themselves build ministries but help pave the way for spiritual leaders to more effectively minister to their communities, not merely to their congregations. They need not lead nations from the top; but instead influence from below. Like the prophets of the Old Testament, they uncover the hidden aspects of the society, its social, philosophical, psychological and biological problems; in a way that <u>transcends mere morality</u>, but instead is tangible to the entire society. They pave the way for scientists, doctors, inventors, psychologists, etc., to more efficiently perform their duties. They can integrate their wisdom-based understanding into these fields, where as the secularized doctors, scientists, etc., must *through their own worldviews* remain knowledge-based. They understand the value of knowledge <u>and</u> its limitations. Men and women of understanding will unlock, to the world, the reality that the Biblical Worldview is, and can be, the only true worldview of existence, because existence is the stage through which all knowledge is brought forth.

BACK TO THE BEGINNING... FORWARD TOWARD THE END

Although the book of Daniel speaks of these "understanding" individuals, it is the last book in the Bible that seems to provide the reasoning and responsibility for this critical group. As you have now learned, the Bible is clear that wisdom created the earth and mankind in perfection, and that mankind rejected wisdom and chose knowledge, electing not merely to operate – but to seek solutions – wholly inside a post-fall universe. I also have stated that understanding becomes the key between these two realms, pre-fall and post-fall. As men and women of understanding begin to step in and through wisdom transform this post-fall world, they will in essence "rebuild the ancient ruins." (Is. 61:4) At which point, scripture states that God steps in, finalizing a complete "reconciliation."

If this final reconciliation occurs, what then would naturally disappear from existence? To answer that question is to ask what is missing from the book of Revelation? Or perhaps, I should say, what might be the "revelation" of the book of Revelation? Amid all of the radically apocalyptic imagery and hyper-elaborate poetic symbolism of Revelation we find nearly an identical laundry list of items that were present at the beginning of pre-fall creation and also are present at the end of the age. The itemized accounts between the books of Genesis and Revelation (garden, river, serpent, animals, etc.) are exactingly identical, except one – at the end of the age there is no tree of the KNOWLEDGE of good and evil. Knowledge, or our current post-fall operating system, has been removed. As men and women of understanding fulfill their purposes, and God fulfills His promised covenant of reconciliation, the tragedy and trauma of our post-fall, sin-infected and entropic-centered world is eradicated. Existence, which now exists in post-fall state (knowledge), has been reconciled back to its pre-fall state (wisdom and understanding).

This is the time for men and women of understanding to cry out for the benefit and protection of all of God's image on the planet, a time to believe that "every knee shall bow and every tongue confess" in the reality and love of God. And all of existence, stuck under the cataclysmic cycle of post-fall perpetuation (knowledge), and all of heaven (wisdom), eager to see the fulfillment of its wondrous intent (understanding), is waiting:

God will see God's own primal dream for creation finally coming true - - and that dream won't be imposed by God from outside by domination against creation's will, but it will emerge from within creation itself, so that God's dream and creation's groaning for fulfillment will be one. (Brian D. McLaren, The Secret Message of Jesus, p. 203)

In the final chapter, you'll discover just how critically important this time in history becomes in the propagation of this wondrous opportunity.

Chapter 26

OUR MISSION CRITICAL HOUR

Ponder:
As you <u>do not know</u> the path of the wind, or how the body is formed in a mother's womb, so you cannot understand the work of God, the Maker of all things.
(Eccl. 11:5, NIV, underline mine)

The passage above is a fascinating one, especially if we remove it from its historical point in time. At the time the Israelites were given these words, this passage would have bespoken the infinite wonder of God by elucidating how they couldn't understand how He had designed His creation. At the time, it evoked awesome reverence. But we have to realize that this scripture was inspired by the Holy Spirit and written so that we, millennia after it was first inscribed, could hear these words for ourselves. Why is this important, especially for our particular moment in historical time?

Because we do now know the path of the wind and we now understand how the body is formed in the mother's womb....

The first successful weather satellite was TIROS-1. It was launched by NASA on April 1, 1960. TIROS was the frontrunner to most of the Earth-observing satellites NASA and NOAA subsequently have launched. These satellites accomplish some very particular assignments. Consider the following quote from Wikipedia:

Visible-light images from weather satellites during local daylight hours are easy to interpret even by the average person; clouds, cloud systems such as fronts and tropical storms, lakes, forests, mountains, snow ice, fires, and pollution such as smoke, smog, dust and haze are readily apparent. <u>Even wind can be determined</u> by cloud patterns, alignments

and movement from successive photos.
(http://en.wikipedia.org/wiki/Weather_satellite)

We also have been able to peer into the body using ultrasound machines and, like the weather satellite, that technology is well less than a century old. The ultrasound machine was first used as a medical tool on the human body in the late 1940s. But the computer technology to enhance ultrasound imagery was introduced in 1979 by Samuel H. Maslak. We've become *even more detailed* at peering into the human body during full function since then. Instead of just understanding the internal body in motion, we now can observe *how the body thinks*. Technologies such as Positron Emission Tomography (PET) and functional magnetic resonance imaging (fMRI) allow scientists and doctors to peer into the brain as it processes thoughts and actions. While ultrasound already allows us to see how the bones are formed in the womb, PET and fMRI technology uncover how the brain functions during formation and action.

So why is this important? How is this relevant to a verse written millennia prior to this moment in time? Because if we take this verse in Ecclesiastes and add in the logic that, "If A=B and B=C, then A=C," then we can rewrite the verse in the following manner:

Just as you now know the path of the wind, and how the body is formed in a mother's womb, so you now understand the work of God, the Maker of all things.

Now, before I continue, I did not say that because of these technologies we understand God. That is a mystery that science, academics and religion will never discover. He is omnipotent and omnipresent – He cannot be fully known by man. Thankfully, as we have seen in the book, relationship and participation in His storyline open us up to deeper revelation. But we can now, at this moment in time, most fully understand the "work" of God. And (carefully analyzing the phrasing from our verse above) we can understand God, as the "Maker of all things," with our greatest historical clarity.

How?

Because of the historical clarity of science.

Wait a minute: as science has progressed, its naturalistic ambassadors *appear* to refute God with more and more certainty. But in fact, shoving all ideological presuppositions aside, the exact opposite has occurred. For science is a study of *reaction*. We use our research tools to determine the cause and effect after any action has been committed. What we observe after those moments of action is called science. And the more advanced our technologies, the closer the time between action and reaction merges. Let me give you an example with tobacco smoking. For centuries, science has been able to determine through autopsies that the devastated black lungs of a smoker are the direct result of his habitual smoking habit. Forty years ago, we could create an internal snapshot of the lungs through an X-ray machine and show a living man how cigarettes had impacted his body over the length of his habit.

Twenty years ago, we could see how cigarette smoke entered the body and observe its immediate effects on the lungs and other organs. Ten years or so ago, we uncovered how at the moment the first puff of smoke enters the mouth, nicotine enters the brain, causing the brain to release the neurotransmitters dopamine, acetylcholine and glutamate across the brain's synaptic pathways, creating a sense of euphoria and physiologically accelerating the addiction process. From the first inhalation, the body is pushing toward addiction and thereby leading the body toward cancer, emphysema, heart disease and stroke. As I already have stated in previous chapters, we now can see how these outcomes are the *deliberate* intent of these actions.

Instead of just *knowing* that smoking kills, we now can expose *the strategies* of the process.

In the same manner, we now can mine new and relevant depths to God's post-fall law declarations and many of the statements made by Christ. We now can even deeper understand why Jesus said, "Anyone who looks at a woman lustfully has already committed adultery with her in his heart," because of how the brain reacts at the moment of visual arousal. We can see why Paul would declare that a war rages within his members, because of how the brain builds up and strengthens synaptic pathways based on the pleasurable aspect of certain actions. We have new revelation into Jesus' statement, "Be slow to anger," because we can see in real time the effects of anger on the heart, brain and other organs.

We can see how promiscuous sex among young people deliberately leads to cervical cancer, based on how sperm imprint themselves into the human body. We can see that through drug usage such as meth, the body lowers dopamine levels in the brain after the first intake, and from that moment forward, the only thing that once again leads back to normal, healthy dopamine levels is... meth. We can see how charity and selflessness lead to better brain chemistry, increase mood and function and promote organ health.

We now can see that God's creations, such as fruits, vegetables and fish are not only beneficial for sustaining life, but also that the natural compounds and enzymes in many foods immediately benefit areas of the brain, heart, lungs and eyes. We can see that these same foods are important for skin and follicle health. We can see that fish oils such as Omega 3 accelerate learning and brain function and health. The examples go on and on. You just need to know how to look.

Bottom line, we can now understand more of *the work of God*, because we now have the technologies to understand how He created us *("the Maker of all things")* to function from the *moment* of any action.

This is what God was attempting to do through that small nomadic nation of Israel. The rest of the world wasn't going to come to an understanding of Him through the initial actions of the Israelites, but through the <u>consequential reactions</u> that were to follow. The beneficial consequences of their actions were to expose the ways of God, and then God Himself, to the rest of the world.

As we see in scripture, the Israelites failed. But we don't have to.

I hope as you have read this book, you have gained a deeper understanding of the criticality of this hour in the vast span of history. This final chapter is meant to solidify that discovery. As believers at this moment in linear time, we have an incredible opportunity and an immense responsibility. Our job is not to prove our worldview, or lord it over others. Our mandate is to understand the magnitude of what we have been given (the Biblical Worldview and all its promises); how immense and loving our Creator God truly is; whom we are to partner with (God, Christ, His Spirit and other believers); and to whom our focus and love should be showered upon (humanity).

I'll leave you with one final set of verses. The first verse carries massive significance for me. So much so, that I attempted (and failed) to build an organization around the declaration.

> *Those who have insight will shine brightly like the brightness of the expanse of heaven, and those who lead the many to righteousness, like the stars forever and ever. But as for you, Daniel, conceal these words and seal up the book until the end of time; many will go back and forth, and knowledge will increase.* (Dan. 12:3-4, NASB)

What an amazing passage verse 3 is! It is an ultimate moment of the salvation of many through those with "insight." As Christ would say, it occurs through those who have ears that can "hear" and eyes that can "see." For years I relished in this verse. Then on a trip down to Brazil with a pastor friend of mine, I spent time with our host pastor's father, a very wise man. Though he knew little English and I knew less Portuguese, we did our best to communicate. As we attempted to talk I shared with him this verse. With wisdom in his eyes, he looked back at me and said, "But verse 3 is contingent on verse 4." I had read less of verse 4, so I grabbed my bible and read. The words shot through me like a taser:

... [A]nd _knowledge_ will increase.

In verse 3, Daniel was given a prophetic declaration of a time to come, a moment that he could not realize, that for him, must be "sealed up in a book." Why? Because in Daniel's day, knowledge hadn't reached the level necessary for these revelations. Science hadn't caught up yet. The _works_ of God could not be better known, because we couldn't understand how God had "fashioned" us. But we can in this hour.

Verse 3 wasn't Daniel's hour, but it just may be ours.

I hope this book has inspired you to see the wondrous magnitude of the worldview you possess. But these discovers aren't just meant for you to internalize. It's now time for you to carry these revelations forward. To not only see the factuality of your worldview, but also the responsibility it carries. The tools are available, the landscape is ready and the fields are ripe for "harvest." Let us become the generation spoken of in Daniel 12:3 by understanding the magnitude of our Daniel 12:4 moment.

Live inspired.

24178700R00093

Made in the USA
Charleston, SC
14 November 2013